Casebooks on Economic Principles

GOVERNMENT AND MARKETS

Andrew Leake
Head of Economics
Latymer Upper School, Hammersmith

Macmillan Education

First published 1983

Published by
MACMILLAN EDUCATION LIMITED
Houndmills Basingstoke Hampshire RG21 2XS
and London
Associated companies throughout the world

Printed in Hong Kong

British Library Cataloguing in Publication Data

Leake, Andrew
Government and markets. — (Casebooks on economic
principles)
1. Supply and demand 2. Economic policy
I. Title
338.5 HB201

ISBN 0-333-27990-5

Contents

1   Introduction   5

2   Welfare and efficiency
2.1   Free or controlled   6
2.2   The reasons for government intervention   8
2.3   Public goods and services   10

3   Market imperfections
3.1   Market clearing   12
3.2   Market dominance   14
3.3   Social cost and benefit   16

4   Taxation
4.1   Taxes and welfare   18
4.2   Taxes and efficiency   20
4.3   The burden of taxation   22

5   Stocks
5.1   The problems of agriculture   24
5.2   Buffer stocks   27

6   Public ownership
6.1   State enterprise   30
6.2   Nationalisation   31

7   Public sector pricing
7.1   Private and social accounts   34
7.2   Pricing for efficiency   36
7.3   Price discrimination   38

8   Public investment
8.1   Private and social returns   40
8.2   Cost-benefit analysis   42

Suggested answers   44

Sources   46

Index   47

Acknowledgements

The author and publishers wish to thank the following who have kindly given permission for the use of copyright material:

Edward Arnold (Publishers) Limited for an extract from *The Process of Industrialization 1750-1870, Vol 1.* in the *Documents of European Economic History* series, by Pollard and Holmes;

British Telecom for an extract from the leaflet *Telephone Charges;*

Commission des Communautés Européennes for an extract from *European Community*

The Controller of Her Majesty's Stationery Office for an extract from *Room to Expand* issued by the Department of Trade;

The Financial Times Business Information Limited for articles published in *The Financial Times*: 'Patent Law Changes', 25 April 1975; 'Diazo Price Ring Rap' 3 March 1977; 'When taxes are good for your health' 16 February 1978, and 'Whitby's mine of uncertainty' 16 February 1978;

Guardian Newspapers Limited for the articles 'A Streetcar named Despair' by Barry Norman and 'Rail Fares Up' by Jane McLoughlin, 29 December 1979;

Irish Academic Press for a table and diagram from *Principles of Farm Business: Analysis and Management* by R O'Connor (1973);

The Labour Party, for an extract from a Statement by the NEC, Blackpool 1976;

Lloyds Bank Limited for extracts from 'The Future of the Nationalized Industries' by John Redwood, *Lloyds Bank Review* October 1976; 'Taxation and Incentives in the UK' by Michael Beenstock, *Lloyds Bank Review* October 1979, and 'Business's Turn for Tax Cuts' *Lloyds Bank Economic Bulletin* February 1980;

London Express News and Feature Services for the extract 'The Biggest Boss in Britain' published in the *Sun,* 12 June 1981;

Tim Malyon, Legalise Cannabis Campaign, for his letter in *The Sunday Times,* 9 July 1978;

Lord Robbins for an extract from *The Economic Problem in Peace and War,* Macmillan, 1957;

Brian Slater for his letter in *The Times,* 22 February 1978;

Syndication International Ltd for the article 'Giveawayday' published in the *Daily Mirror* 12 June 1978;

Times Newspapers Limited for the article 'Is West Germany's Post Office misusing its monopoly?' from *The Times* 8 February 1980; and articles from *The Sunday Times* 'Reviving industry or £3bn workhouse?' 19 March 1978;

'Trailing to fitness' 24 September 1978; 'The cost of cleaning up America' 22 October 1972; 'Every cloud has a silver lining' 17 September 1978; 'Brazilians explain why coffee will never be cheap again' 25 September 1977; 'Market set to sell off surplus wine to Russians' 21 September 1975, and 'Switch from rail to road' 1 February 1976.

Every effort has been made to trace all the copyright holders but if any have been inadvertently overlooked the publishers will be pleased to make the necessary arrangement at the first opportunity.

1 Introduction

Theory and practice

Learning to drive a car is not easy. You may read all the books, be told what to do by your instructor, and still not be able to do it all by yourself. It takes theory and practice, together.

So it is with economics. The theory explains in general terms what should be happening. It takes all possibilities into account. It can be learned from teachers or from textbooks.

For most of us, however, the appeal of economics lies in the practical side of the subject. Just as we want to be able to drive a car for ourselves, so we want to be able to consider and understand the economic problems we see in the real world. It is the purpose of this, and the other Casebooks, to consider theory and practice, side by side.

Stage by stage

You have to do many different things to drive a car. You have to control the steering, the accelerator, the brakes and the gears. Although you will use them all together in the end, it helps if you can try them one at a time, at the start.

It is the same with economic theory. We need to understand many different ideas, and the connections between them. By taking ideas one at a time, from each area of the subject in turn, we will eventually have built up a complete picture.

So it is the approach in this, and the other Casebooks, to study each important principle in a separate section, and to consider economics stage by stage.

How to use this Casebook

Each section considers a particular aspect of economic behaviour. It does this in three ways. First there is a brief outline of the general principles involved. Next there is an illustration of the way those principles apply in the real world. Finally there are questions based on the issues raised in the section, and arising from the material studied.

The outline of theory is a concise summary of work that has already been covered. It does not develop the general theory to any great depth, but restates and reinforces the most important aspects of each economic principle. It aims to provide a complete preparation for all that follows in the section, and in the rest of the Casebook.

The applications are of individual principles, rather than of broad topics. Their use will be in making practical sense of abstract ideas, and in providing examples to illustrate theoretical points. They are the sort of decisions that are made by individuals and governments each day: things that matter to all of us.

It is hoped that this material will be of interest both for its economic content and in its own right.

Government and markets

Governments are elected to protect the collective interests of their citizens. The policies they adopt in order to do so arise from causes that are political, social and economic. Difficult though it may be, we will try here to ignore subjective matters, and to consider only the economic responsibilities of government.

We will study the principles of policy, but not the details and the developments that refer to particular cases. This will construct a general framework of ideas with which we can hope to understand more fully the purposes and effects of intervention, wherever it is found.

Governments intervene in many different areas of the economy. Much of their involvement is in macro-economic matters, and their policies are intended to affect the general levels of output, employment and prices. The principles behind this intervention are considered elsewhere, in the Casebook on Macroeconomics.

In all that follows our interest is in the intervention of government in individual decisions, in the many distinct markets of the economy. There are many reasons for influencing supply and demand in many different markets, and many different ways of doing so. These policies, and their effects on the markets concerned, are studied here.

2 Welfare and efficiency

individuals will decide the issue, or the state will take command and decide priorities on a collective basis.

This distinction applies most strongly to the divide between the western, free enterprise economies of the world and the eastern communist block. It is also an issue that must be faced by an economy such as Britain's in the very different conditions of peace and war.

2.1 Free or controlled

'The economic problem in peace and war'

There is a fundamental problem that must be solved by any economy. Resources are limited in relation to unlimited wants for the goods and services that can be produced. Decisions must be made, therefore, as to which wants are to be satisfied, and in which order.

There are many different forms of economic system, and in each of them decisions are taken in a different way. They tend, however, to one or other of two extremes: either the market behaviour of free

Efficiency

Free enterprise allows resources to be matched to wants, on the basis of individual decisions. The owners of factors of production supply them to firms wanting to employ resources, and the price mechanism matches supply and demand in each factor market. The problem of a shortage of labour to serve in the armed services should be solved by a rise in relative pay or in forms of job satisfaction.

Firms use their factors to produce goods and services for sale in product markets. Consumers buy this output at a price set to match supply and demand, and to satisfy their wants. Firms increase their supply of goods in response 'to a financial

The economic problem in peace and war

In total war there is only one prime object of policy, the achievement of total victory. To that object all other aims are subordinate, by that criterion all special operations must be judged. . . .

In such circumstances the major problem of allocation, the allocation of resources between private and public consumption, undergoes a most drastic simplification. . . .

Consider first the manning of the armed forces. . . . I wonder whether, at this time of day, there is anyone who would seriously argue that it would have been wise to rely on voluntary recruitment. It is quite true, as I expect many of you who have been conscripted are thinking, that the market system was not put to a very severe test. Rates of pay were not raised so as greatly to increase the differential attraction of service. Doubtless, if they had been raised enough, many more would have been tempted in. But would it have been prudent to rely upon this incentive? . . .

Similar considerations apply to the use of material resources. Reliance upon a voluntary response to a financial incentive is reasonable enough when the response needed is small in relation to the total national resources. But when it is essential that the response shall be total — that no resources which could be useful remain unused — or put to uses that

are not essential — it is not enough. Powers must be taken to commandeer and direct the use of stocks, plants, land and means of transport, and, if necessary, to prohibit their use for other purposes. . . .

So much for the conditions of supply. But what about the mechanism for the allocation of resources? Here, too, conditions are completely different from anything which is assumed in the peace-time models. . . . The competitors in the market, or some of them at any rate, are working to government orders. So far as they are concerned, credit is virtually unlimited. . . . There is, therefore, virtually no limit on the possible upward movement of prices. . . .

In such circumstances recourse is had to price fixing. But if the mechanism of the market is thus paralysed, it is necessary to provide other means for the performance of its functions. . . .

We must not exaggerate the degree of efficiency of our wartime arrangements and improvisations. The degree of waste and misdirection was doubtless such that if any but the highest stakes of all had been at issue, this kind of cost alone would have been judged to be prohibitive. But the end was not wholly an accident. 'The reason you won and we lost', the wretched Speer is reported to have said, 'was that you made total war and we did not.'

[*The author of the book from which this extract is taken would like it said that it by no means represents his final word on the subject.*]

incentive' from price and profit, and consumers decide their demand on the basis of relative prices and their limited income.

If all goes well each of these decisions is made in the most efficient way. Factors are employed so that their productivity is related to price, goods are sold so that the opportunity cost of their production is related to price, and consumers buy goods so that price relates to their level of satisfaction. The free market system achieves the most suitable match of resources to wants.

Welfare

The individual decisions of producers and consumers do not always serve their collective interests. In times of peace it may be possible to adjust the working of the market system in order to overcome this difficulty, but in times of war things are rather different. The welfare of the population becomes dependent upon only one issue, 'the achievement of total victory'. If the free market cannot serve this wider objective with absolute consistency it must be replaced by direct controls.

Now resources are matched to wants in a different way, and with a different outcome. Factors are directed to particular employments and labour is conscripted into the armed services. Firms are directed to produce goods that are needed for the war effort, and measures taken to 'prohibit their use for other purposes'. Demand which would be unlimited if backed by limitless state credit is replaced by price-fixing and rationing. The state directs the allocation of goods to individual consumers.

War introduces a 'most drastic simplification'. In a more complex market economy these issues must be tackled in rather different ways. The free market must be left, and even assisted, to allow individuals to make their decisions in an efficient way. In areas where this fails to serve the welfare of the community as a whole it is for society to find ways of intervening in the market to correct the imbalance.

'Drugs: the prohibition effect'

The power of the market is so strong that even the most vigorous controls cannot be certain of restraining its pressures indefinitely. In time of war, it is common for 'black market' economies to prosper as individual producers and consumers continue to trade to their mutual advantage. Whenever buyers and sellers wish to exchange a commodity in this way it is very difficult to prevent them.

Even the force of law may not fully restrain the ability of free enterprise forces to match resources to wants. If there are indeed '15 million' consumers of a good, with demand worth \$4 billion, suppliers will have a major incentive to supply that market. Prohibition may only increase the rewards that can be earned by doing so.

Cannabis ban only puts up prices

It is now 50 years since the first international treaty and the first British laws prohibiting cannabis came into effect. Talking of the four and 21-ton cannabis smuggling runs, last week's Sunday Times Insight article on the Moroccan hash trade demonstrated clearly that international trade has not been seriously curtailed by these laws. Nor is it likely to be while there is such well-established demand and no legal source of supply.

In the USA alone, according to government-sponsored surveys, there are 15 million regular cannabis users, 8 per cent of the adult population, consuming at least \$4 billion worth between them. At a conservative estimate there are one to two million regular users in this country.

It is unlikely that the arrest of a single large supplier such as Krop would have any significant impact on the market. The effect of putting major suppliers out of business will only be to create temporary scarcity which will increase prices and thereby increase the incentive for new operators to enter the business. This is the classic prohibition effect which was seen most clearly in the case of alcohol prohibition in the USA.

Whatever the moral and medical arguments of the case, the power of free market forces is clearly not to be denied.

QUESTIONS

(i)   In wartime, the free market allows resources to be put to uses that are 'not essential'. Why is this?

(ii)   What non-monetary advantages and disadvantages prevent labour from following normal market pressures when joining the armed services in wartime?

(iii)   By what argument might a 'legal source of supply' be said to limit sales more effectively than prohibition?

(iv)   Draw a supply and demand diagram of a 'black market', showing the effect of both the arrest of certain suppliers and fines imposed on consumers.

2.2 The reasons for government intervention

The problems of government have changed little through the ages. In Imperial Rome, for instance, Nero was well used to the inconvenience of having to decide a man's fate in the arena. A gladiator would stand poised, sword held high above his vanquished enemy. Had the crowd been well entertained? Should the fallen gladiator be spared to fight another day? Only the Emperor could decide, and having decided he would give the sign — thumbs up, or thumbs down!

The gladiators use more sophisticated economic weapons now, and the authorities must base their decisions on more complicated research. They would also claim, although not without dispute, to make their judgements with more responsibility than the Emperor Nero!

One major characteristic, however, they do have in common. A government will still choose to intervene in a free market for one of two broad and opposite reasons: either to help the market in its work, or to hinder it. Either 'thumbs up', or 'thumbs down'.

For or against the market?

On the one hand the government may approve of the outcome of market forces, believing the outcome to be in the best interests of the community. If there is some imperfection in the process, the government may intervene to try to repair the fault. Examples of this approach might include the work of the Department of Trade to inform business about commercial opportunities overseas, or of the Bank of England to smooth out transitory fluctuations in the exchange rate of the pound sterling.

On the other hand, the government may object to the outcome of free market forces, even when the market is working as well as it can. They may feel that individuals are failing to take account of the wider effects of their actions upon the community. Policies to reflect this concern include the control of pollution through fines, and the provision of a welfare state.

'Reviving industry, or £3 billion workhouse?'

The huge sum paid by the government to British industry is given in many different ways, and for various reasons. In fact, as we can see, some of those reasons stand in opposition to one another!

One hand seems to have its thumb well up. To revive industry is the objective, and measures such as

Reviving industry or £3bn workhouse?

In the financial year now closing the Government will have spent some £2.5bn on aid to industry and employment — not counting unemployment benefit.

Except to the extent that it increases productivity, this is a direct cost to us as consumers. We could otherwise be paying lower taxes and have that much greater take-home pay. Why do we do it? And is the money well spent?

The main aims are to increase investment and to reduce unemployment. Beyond that, there is also a good deal of cosseting of certain kinds of advanced technology which is presumably expected to pay off eventually, and somewhat over £200m a year is being spent on about a dozen individual rescue operations, of which British Leyland is the most costly....

Last week I argued that Britain's regional problems had arisen largely from poor adaptation to the gradual loss of advantage in international trade by industries in those areas. (There were other causes too, of course, such as inadequate skills and the tendency of educated people to move away.)...

That perspective on the problem would suggest that industrial policy should be occupied with assisting the switch from declining industries to ones with growth potential, rather than pursuing the present mixed bag of policies and objectives. One cannot however take such a purist approach. In the steel industry, for example, it would suggest going for a drastic contraction which is not feasible socially. There the best policy is obviously to close as many uneconomic works as possible, and invest to raise productivity in the rest. (Last week the Government decided not to

redundancy payments, retraining programmes, and investment in new growth industries all further this end. They assist the market system in encouraging industry to adapt to meet changing patterns of demand, and to produce goods that will sell successfully in a free market.

At the same time, the government's other hand seems to have its thumb pointing down. The government is trying to resist the forces of the market, by subsidising industries that are in decline, and by preventing the rearrangement of factors of production. Much of the finance given to industry is in the form of subsidies for the employment of both labour and capital in so-called 'lame ducks'. Clearly the government is concerned to protect the community from the social and economic hardships of unemployment, and the further depression of poorer regions, but it does lay itself open to the accusation that it is do that either.)

But the pre-eminent need — for firms and workers to adjust and change to activities which will make a profit — should be kept firmly in mind. It is time for the Government to have a fundamental rethink of its industrial policies.

Ideally, the only such policies would be redundancy payments and retraining, to assist workers to shift to more productive jobs. . . .

That apart, the main trend in this Government's policy has been towards more selective, case-by-case assistance. . . .

There are dangers in this: political influence, distortions of competition (as between firms in assisted areas), and promotion of activities with low productivity. The administrators of the policy contend that they are always mindful of these dangers, and on the charge of supporting poor productivity, which seems to me the most widespread of the three risks, they contend that in general any apparent subsidy to poor performance is due to the start-up costs of assisted projects, which are, however, expected to be as profitable and productive as competing ones in the long run. . . .

Then there are the rescues. The policy now is to avoid bailing out failed firms where possible. . . .

As international competition intensifies, such cases are likely to become more numerous. While I have no instant solution, it does seem necessary for the Government, in treating with these problems, to take a clear view at an early stage as to whether it is backing a turn-around (which tends to cost a lot of money) or providing indoor welfare, a twentieth-century version of the Victorian workhouse. It is a distinction which has not always been made in the past.

This might even be a tactic to appeal to the Emperor Nero — to grant the loser his life temporarily, while building up his gladiators' strength for battles in the future?

QUESTIONS

(i) Explain the possible market imperfections which can be overcome by (a) commercial advice from the Department of Trade, (b) support for the exchange rate by the Bank of England.

(ii) Why is British industry not able to meet changes in demand and supply without government support?

(iii) What is the effect on the market for advanced technology of government 'cosseting'?

(iv) What would happen to government spending on industry in the long term if it succeeded in (a) helping market forces to restructure production, (b) preventing market pressures from coming to bear?

(v) How does the government policy towards industry that is described here affect the distribution of income?

sponsoring a '£3 billion workhouse'.

This distinction, between financing adjustment to market forces or resisting the process of decline in industry, is one which 'has not always been made in the past'. How then might the government justify its apparently inconsistent approach?

A policy for growth

The answer lies in the *timing* of each part of the policy. Even with large support from the state, the processes of growth, readjustment, and development take a long time. Without government protection the market would cause widespread unemployment and decline in the meantime. Provided the 'thumbs down' policy plays only a temporary part in the government's plans, it can still succeed with its 'thumbs up' approach of encouraging development.

2.3 Public goods and services

Certain goods and services give satisfaction to consumers but cannot be supplied under conditions of free enterprise. Services such as street lighting, water purification, and footpaths cannot benefit one consumer without also benefiting all others. No individual feels that he need spend his income on these benefits when he can have unlimited access to them for free. No producer can make a profit by selling them, and supply must be offered collectively, by associations or governments. Collective self-interest requires that there should be state enterprise, and that it should supply public goods and services to all consumers together.

How is this supply to be paid for? Individual pricing will not succeed for the state any more than for free enterprise. Instead there must be some general and compulsory payment by all members of society. Those who benefit collectively from the goods and services provided will pay for them, as fairly and efficiently as possible, in general taxation.

'Trailing to fitness'

'Jogging, walking and cycling' take place in the main in public places. There is open access to the general public, and it is not possible to prevent their use by 'free-loaders' at the same time as charging for their use by particular individuals. The provision of parkland, open country, tracks and minor roads is a service which is generally best left to the state.

'Trim trails' are a similar case. These are tracks constructed in open places, with equipment such as parallel bars and handles placed at intervals. Members of the general public can exercise on this course and, whatever it may feel like at the time, benefit as a result.

With open access it is not possible to prevent those you do not wish to pay for the service from using it. One individual could buy a 'trim trail' for his own use, but would need to be willing to allow others to benefit from it also. Not very many would be provided on this basis.

Public supply

Public goods are those where, if one person benefits, all others share those benefits. A similar but less extreme case applies to many more goods and services. This is when benefits are shared by society, although not perhaps as much as they are enjoyed by the individual. The goods and services that offer these benefits can be provided by free enterprise, but their added merit to the state encourages some measure of public supply as well.

Sports facilities are often of this kind. Golf courses, squash, tennis courts, swimming pools, and athletics tracks can be run as private companies supported by government, or as government services supported by commercial trading. In both ways it is possible to gain the private and social benefits offered by such facilities.

A mixed economy provides many of the basic services of life on this basis. Health care, education, power and social security, are all areas where social responsibility is given weight alongside commercial efficiency. The wide influence which this gives government can be used for social and political purposes, as well as the purely economic. It does, however, offer an opportunity to protect the welfare of the community.

'A Streetcar Named Despair'

Emergency services could be provided by free enterprise. Consumers would pay a price for the services they required, and that price would be set by supply and demand. The more serious the injury, the more inconvenient the time, or the more desperate the danger, the greater would be the price!

In practice, of course, the free enterprise system would find a way around these embarrassments. Individuals would take out insurance policies to cover

---

Trailing to fitness

Last week the chairman of the Sports Council, exhorted more of his fellow countrymen and women to try their hand at trim trails and other physical exercise when he introduced his Council's 'Sport for All – Come Alive' campaign.

The theory of the trim trail is simple enough: you jog round a marked trail and stop at intervals to participate in exercises that require no supervision. Any local authority worth its salt can build one. The trim trail is part of a broader proposal, however, which argues that the more people who jog, swim, cycle, walk and generally exercise, the less we, as a nation, will spend on curing the illnesses caused by inactivity.

This is not a new theory, it simply has been taking time to sink into Britain's national consciousness. In West Germany, for example, studies have already shown how health can be improved by exercise programmes and (TUC please note) even incomes can be improved. 'It is clear,' says the conclusion of a report commissioned by the Sports Council from Professor Peter Fentem, 'that exercise can be of considerable benefit to everyone both physically and mentally, and should be seen as a necessary element in the pattern of daily living at all ages.' Well said.

A Streetcar Named Despair

And so the year draws to its close with the nation heading ever more rapidly towards bankruptcy, the social services plunged into decay, doctors in national health hospitals squabbling fiercely over whose turn it is to use the stethoscope and comprehensive schools faced with closure unless the PTA can find enough money to buy another bit of chalk.

This being so I've been wondering whatever happened to a splendid idea put forward a few weeks ago in a report wherein the GLC proposed to ask the Government for 'wide-ranging powers to charge the public for its services.'

One suggestion, for example, was that people trapped in crashed vehicles should pay the Fire Brigade for rescuing them. Now this introduction of an element of private enterprise into the essential services struck me as such a brilliant, yet simple, wheeze, that I'm astonished we've heard no more about it.

After all, why should people careless enough to get themselves trapped in cars – or anywhere else for that matter – expect the overburdened ratepayer to fork out for the cost of rescue? The GLC's notion makes far better economic sense . . .

One imagines the scene in Oxford Street: wrecked car lying on its roof in Selfridge's window; helpless driver peering out, desperate and upside down; fire engine arriving with clanging bell.

The senior fire officer steps forward. 'Now then, young Alf,' he says to his assistant. 'Leave this to me. There's a bit of tricky negotiation to be gone into here.'

He taps loudly on windscreen to attract attention of semi-conscious driver. 'Whatho, squire. In a right two-and-eight there, aren't you? Well, listen carefully:

nod once if you want us to get you out, twice if you're ready to pay.

'What do you reckon that was, Alf – two nods or a convulsion? Take it as two nods, shall we? Okay, squire, now this bit's very important: can you move your arms? Good, good. Well, slide your hand into your pocket – easy, easy, don't rock the bloody car, whatever you do. Well done. Now – throw out your wallet.

'Got it, Alf? Right. Hand it over.' He opens wallet, draws sharp breath, shakes head, sucks teeth, and taps on windscreen again. 'You gotta do better than this, squire. I mean, a bleedin' fiver – is that all you got? We wouldn't rescue your cat from the top of the wardrobe for that. Oy! Don't pass out on me now, we've got business to discuss.

'Is there anyone we can phone who's liable to come up with the readies? Your mum perhaps? It'll be . . . let's see, there's us and the ambulance people – they'll want bunging, too – tell you what, make you a special price, being as its Christmas: seventy-five knicker all in.

'Who do you know'll cough up that lot? Think about it – only don't take too long because, ask me, that petrol tank's ready to explode. What? . . . Hang on a minute, squire. What's that, Alf? Bloke trapped in a lift in Regent Street? Don't bother me with that now, son. I know all about the bloke in the lift in Regent Street. We'll just leave him there a bit. Suffers something terrible from claustrophobia, he does. Rescue price is going up every minute.

'Now then, squire . . . Oh dear, passed right out, he has. Tell you what, Alf, we'll leave him and we'll leave the bloke in the lift and go have a word with the feller trapped in his lorry in Piccadilly. Been there two days already and he's still haggling over the price. Bit of luck we might just clinch the deal tonight. . . . '

their risks, or would be supported by the charity of others. But what of those who could not find support? The social responsibility of society requires it to offer them security. And what of the danger and inconvenience to others of having wrecks, fires, or the injured lying untended by the roadside? The benefits shared by the rest of society make it worthwhile, collectively, to offer free essential services.

QUESTIONS

(i)   What benefits to society, besides those to private customers, explain the government's support of industry?

(ii)   How does one individual's good health benefit others?

(iii)   Explain whether it is fair to regard public goods as charity.

(iv)   The Sports Council is a government-funded body, seeking to promote sport and to represent sporting interests. Does it provide a public service?

(v)   'Why should people trapped in cars expect the ratepayer to fork out for the cost of rescue?' How would you answer?

3 Market Imperfections

3.1 Market clearing

The government intervenes in the market system because, in broad terms, it wishes either to help the market do its work, or to prevent the results of free enterprise. We will begin here to study the first of these issues, and ask why the market should need help in order to match supply with demand, and what the government might be able to offer.

Supply and demand in any market are each set by a number of different influences. The market system arranges that any difference between them, one way or the other, is cleared through changes in market price. If there is excess demand, price will rise, and if there is excess supply, price will fall (see Diagram 1).

If this process is to work satisfactorily, however, certain conditions must be met. Those dealing in the market must know about the true state of supply and demand, and must be motivated to change their behaviour whenever there is a change in price. In addition to this, it must be possible for price to change freely. If any of these conditions fails to apply in a particular market, an excess of supply or demand will tend to persist. It is then that the government might be able to assist, by increasing knowledge, motivation, or freedom within the market.

'Room to expand'

Part of the reason for decline in the regions of Britain is that there is a lack of knowledge, on the part of businessmen, about the opportunities that are available. There is an ample supply of land for development, of labour to employ, and of resources to offer a good quality of life. In this sense there is an excess supply of factors available in the 'Development Areas' compared with excess demand in the South East and Midlands.

The government has tried to overcome this lack of knowledge by issuing publications, from one of which this extract is taken. They have also introduced an 'Industrial Expansion service to provide information and practical help'. In this way they might help the market system to solve in part the problems of the depressed regions.

'Patent law changes'

In many fields of industry, and in chemicals in particular, it takes many years to develop new products. Market behaviour here takes the form of firms researching into new drugs, which are more successful than their competitors, and which earn profits that justify their development.

The Law of Patents protects firms' investment, and encourages them to make these innovations. Without it, competitors would be able to copy a new

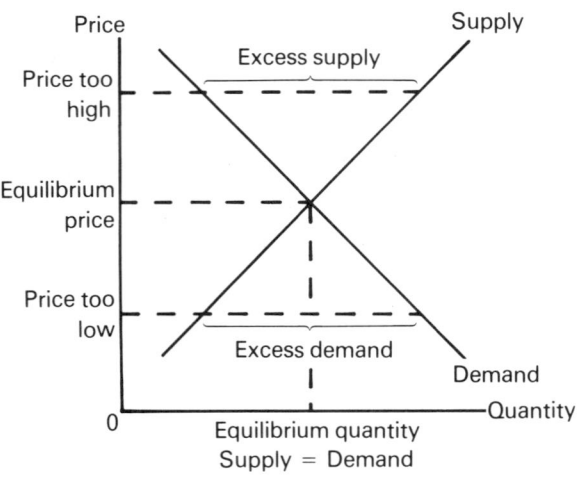

Diagram 1   Market clearing

Room to expand

What are the Development Areas? What have they — and Northern Ireland — to offer the businessman seeking room to expand or wanting to launch a new project?

What Government and local authority services are available to make the move easier and smoother? How would his wife and family take to their new surroundings? What of housing, education and recreation?

The aim of this book is to try to answer these questions; to present a cross-section of life and work in the Development Areas and Northern Ireland. It does not attempt to give a comprehensive picture of what amounts to half the area of Britain.

The businessman will have further questions, individual problems to be solved. The Board of Trade's Industrial Expansion service can provide information and practical help and make arrangements for him to see the Development Areas for himself.

Patent law changes

The recent White Paper on Patent Law Reform is an attempt – albeit belated – to . . . strengthen the commercial protection of inventions. . . .

The White Paper . . . proposes an extension in patent life from 16 years to 20 years as in many other countries.

Although this is an important step for all innovative industries, it has particular relevance to research-intensive sectors like pharmaceuticals and agricultural chemicals. For research is becoming more difficult and expensive as each year passes and it is not impossible for a company spending, say, £10m a year on research and development to go through a decade with nothing to show for it.

Even when a company finds a successful new drug – and it may have to test more than 5000 substances before one reaches the market – it is faced with increasingly stringent controls. As a result it can take eight years or more to develop a product internationally – a big chunk out of a 16-year patent life when a company would be hoping to reap the benefits . . .

drug and not have to share the costs of its development. There would be no motivation for research and no source of improved products.

The government imposes a law to protect companies that have developed new products, and taken out patents as cover. This ensures that only the company that has incurred the costs of research and development can profit from the new drug for a period of years. In this way, the government increases the motivation of firms to search for improvements in their products, and the forces of market competition offer the consumer more choice and quality.

'Diazo price ring rap'

Price-fixing between producers limits the freedom with which market price can adjust supply and demand. 'Excess capacity and declining demand' for the paper that is used in photocopying machines implies that there was excess supply in the industry. Where before there had been 'competitive price cutting' there was now price rigidity imposed by arrangement between the three dominant firms in the industry. The market would not be cleared until price moved freely.

The government takes a firm stand in this type of situation, in order to help the market clearing process. Reference by the Office of Fair Trading to the Restrictive Practices Court would almost certainly force the companies 'to abandon their cartel'. Price would then respond more freely to market forces, and ensure a balance of supply with demand.

Diazo price ring rap

A price-fixing ring has been uncovered by the Monopolies Commission among suppliers of diazo coated paper for copying machines.

A report by the commission published yesterday says that at least three of the four main suppliers made price-fixing agreements between 1968 and 1975. As a result all their list prices and discounts came closely into line, and ended a period of competitive price cutting in the £20m market.

These agreements and bargains were made in an obscure series of telephone calls and meetings between the companies after they saw their profit margins badly eroded by competition.

The report suggests that the companies acted irregularly in failing to register these agreements with the Office of Fair Trading. When such agreements are registered, they are assumed to be against the public interest unless the companies can prove otherwise in court.

In all but 11 of the 3000 restrictive practice agreements registered since 1956, the companies have been forced to abandon their cartel. . . .

The leading company in the field is Ozalid, which supplies more than half the diazo paper used in the UK (52 per cent, in 1974-75). . . . The commission found that Ozalid was in a monopoly position in the supply of diazo papers. But, apart from the complex questions of price fixing which involved other companies, the report concluded that Ozalid's monopoly did not run counter to the public interest. . . .

[It did, however, conclude that] 'On whatever basis Ozalid's profits are considered, the figures show that it has been possible for the company to make profits which we consider to be higher than might have been expected in fully competitive conditions in an industry characterised by excess capacity and declining demand in a period which included some years of general economic recession.'

QUESTIONS

(i) Suggest two ways in which the 'Industrial Expansion service' might be financed. Which would you choose, and why?

(ii) Suggest two ways in which the government could encourage research into new chemicals, apart from patents.

(iii) Explain how 'price-fixing' affects the process of equilibrium in an industry, and the level of profits of dominant firms within it.

(iv) Refer to 'Cannabis ban only puts up prices' on page 7. What imperfections of the free market are described there?

3.2   Market dominance

Governments may object to the outcome of market forces (even when the market is working as well as it can) for political, social or economic reasons. Here we must confine ourselves to the economic objections alone, and consider two main issues. One is the question of social costs and benefits, and that we shall consider in the next section. The other is the question of market dominance by particular buyers and sellers, and how that can harm the interests of the community as a whole.

Dominant buyers and sellers can influence market forces to such an extent that price and quantity are set in their own interests. A firm selling as a monopolist to competitive buyers can limit the number of units for sale, raise the market price, and so make super-normal profit at the expense of his customers (see Diagram 1). A buyer dealing as a monopsonist with competitive sellers can limit the number of units he is willing to buy, lower market price, and so gain greater satisfaction at less cost (see Diagram 2).

In either case, there will be a distortion of market price and quantity, a change in the distribution of income between buyers and sellers, and inefficiency in the way the market matches resources to wants. A monopolist will make his product appear artificially scarce, and a monopsonist will make the goods he buys appear artificially abundant.

The government, in representing the welfare of the whole community, can rightly object to either outcome, and can introduce measures to prevent these distortions.

Is West Germany's Post Office misusing its monopoly?

The announcement by the Deutsche Bundespost (the German Federal Post Office) late last month that it intends to market telephones with extras, such as a built-in answering service, has revived the debate in West Germany about whether the organization is abusing its monopoly.

While Britain questions whether the Post Office should be divested of some of its functions, the problem in the Federal Republic is how to keep the service from expanding its monopolistic position by adding new services in markets already served by private firms.

The Bundespost is a formidable competitor. Germany's largest economic enterprise and Europe's largest service organization, it is the country's biggest employer and by far the biggest spender of capital investment. Because of huge operating surpluses in the telephone business, it has been making a net profit of DM 2000m (about £519m) in each of the past few years, despite a stubborn deficit in traditional postal services.

The Bundespost, which operates banking and bus services besides its monopoly of post and telecommunications, has shown, under Herr Kurt Gscheidle, the Minister of Posts and Telecommunications, virtually entrepreneurial enthusiasm for entering new markets.

In the past months, for instance, it has added

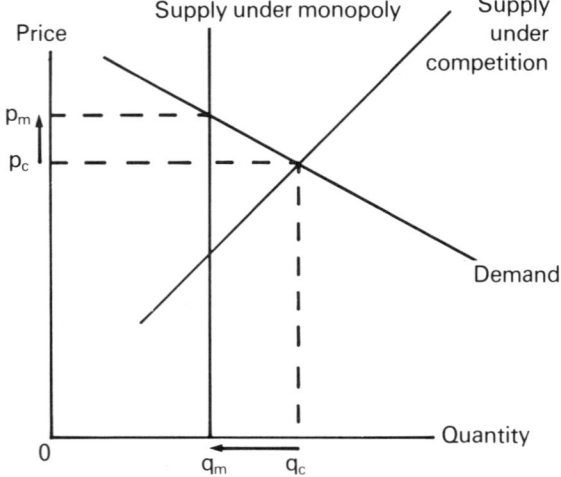

Diagram 1   Monopoly

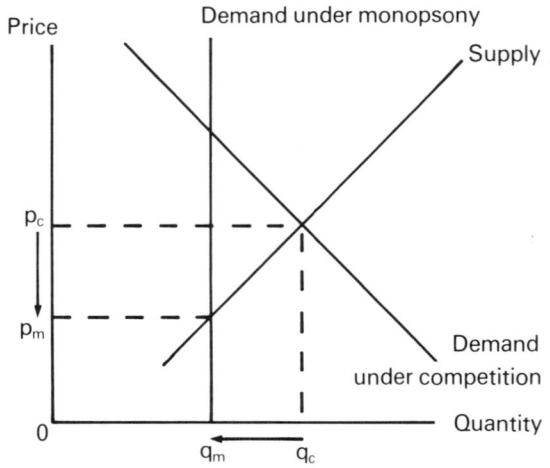

Diagram 2   Monopsony

foreign exchange and traveller's cheques to its banking services. In 1978 it began offering parcel sets for sale, complete with collapsible cardboard box, tape, string and address card – all for as little as one Mark.

These activities, which are clearly outside the Bundespost's monopoly areas, aroused criticism from banks which have always complained that it can undercut them because it does not have to pay postage. Also, stationery shops are resentful that the Bundespost does not have to pay value added tax.

But the main criticism falls on its telecommunications activities especially as new technology opens up fresh sectors. In the past two years the Bundespost has moved into the community aerial and cable television business, the distribution and service of telefacsimile equipment and, now, the marketing of telephone equipment with ancillary electronic functions.

Another charge from the craftsmen was that the Bundespost created an 'information cartel' on technical specifications for community antennae with several large firms which regularly supply telecommunications equipment. This group – most notably Siemens, AEG-Telefunken, Standard Electrik Lorenz (an ITT affiliate), and Philips – are traditional suppliers of telephone and telex equipment.

Small firms not belonging to this group have claimed that they are excluded from Bundespost contracts or prevented from introducing new products.

The latest planned expansion of the service into the supply of specialist telephones has led to new talks with the economics ministry about hindering competition. The Federal Cartel Office in Berlin, which already has several proceedings running against the Bundespost, is also involved in the talks.

'West Germany's Post Office'

An organisation as large as the German Federal Post Office is likely to be dominant in several markets within the economy. In some it will be a dominant seller – it is, for instance, the sole seller protected by law, of postal and telecommunications services. In others it will be a dominant buyer, as, for example, when it buys telecommunications equipment from manufacturers.

Being a state-owned corporation, it would be expected to organise its affairs in the interests of the community as a whole. It will be a matter of great embarrassment to the government if ever it finds that it must control the activities of its own Post Office, to prevent an abuse of market power.

Unfortunately, it is exactly this situation that seems to have come about. The West German Post Office is accused of using its legitimate monopoly power as a supplier of postal services to compete unfairly in 'outside activities'. If it undercuts banks and stationers because it does not need to pay postage and value added tax, it will attract consumers towards its own services. These will appear to be much less expensive and to use fewer resources than is in fact the case.

At the same time it may be using its monopoly position to earn 'huge operating surpluses in the telephone business'. This implies that prices are higher in this field than they need to be.

Lastly it is accused of creating 'an information cartel' in technical areas, buying only from 'several large firms' and excluding smaller ones. This may have allowed it to use its dominant position as a buyer to depress prices below those that reflect the real cost of resources being used in the industry.

In several areas, therefore, it is possible that the Post Office has been making use of its dominant position as 'Germany's largest economic enterprise' to distort prices, and to gain benefits that are not in the interests of the general public. What could the government do about this?

The government is able to restore the balance of market forces, shifting supply or demand through the imposition of taxes or subsidies. A more extreme approach allows them to take supply or demand in a market into state ownership, and so ensure direct control.

In this case, where the offender is already part of the state, it should be possible to introduce corrective measures on the authority of central government. But there may in addition need to be direct investigation and control from those arms of the state that are responsible for competition policy. By advice or enforcement, the 'Federal Cartel Office' may be able to improve the behaviour of the Post Office, and guard the welfare of the community.

QUESTIONS

(i)   A monopolist may be able to produce at lower cost than a competitive industry. How is this? How would it affect Diagram 1? How would it affect government policy?

(ii)   Refer to 'Diazo price ring rap' on page 13. What evidence is there that Ozalid Ltd operated (a) for, (b) against the public interest?

(iii)   How might the German Post Office justify their 'huge operating surpluses in the telephone business'?

(iv)   Describe two imperfections in the market clearing process that are implied by the position of the German Post Office.

3.3 Social cost and benefit

'The cost of cleaning up America'

Pollution is a cost to society that occurs because, in a free market, individuals do not need to take account of all the results of their actions. A ship that dumps waste at sea does so because the private cost of that action is very low. The ship's master does not need to consider the harm his action might do to others who fish, or bathe, or study wildlife in the sea. Only his social conscience, or the controls of government on behalf of society, will bring these issues to his attention.

Thus pollution, in all its many forms, is a social cost. Conversely, we can say that environmental improvements bring social benefits. They may offer little benefit to any particular individual — car manufacturers gain no extra profit from selling cars which produce cleaner exhaust fumes — but they bring benefits to those not directly involved. In a free market individual buyers and sellers need to take account of these benefits, again, only if conscience or government dictate that it should be so.

The social effects of free enterprise

A market system that is based on free enterprise alone takes account of the private costs and private benefits of decisions to the exclusion of social issues.

The cost of cleaning up America

In a matter of only a little over two years, America has gone crazy over its environment. Congress is in a mood to legislate on almost any issue where pollution raises its ugly head. A new water pollution law will mean spending $24 billion of federal money, mostly on improved sewage treatment. It also provides criminal penalties and scope for civil action against industrial polluters who fail to apply the 'best practicable technology' in the abatement of pollution of waterways.

The Administration has recently published some studies of the cost of all this cleanliness. It amounts, all told, to $287 billion over the decade to 1980. This represents an increase of $183 billion over the estimated cost (over the same period) of programmes that were in force in 1970. Most of this cost will be incurred by the private sector, on the principle that 'the polluter must pay.'

In terms of gross national product, this amounts to 2.2%, according to the latest report of the Council on Environmental Quality. This compares with 1.6% estimated in last year's report. The estimates based on 1970 programmes represent just under 1% of GNP.

The figures for environmental costs will certainly get bigger as the decade wears on. For they do not include the cost of several new programmes not yet legislated. These are likely to include: controls on the use of pesticides; curbs on aircraft engine noise, which will involve engine design modifications costing anywhere from $1 billion to $2.7 billion; controls on dumping of wastes at sea by American ships and those calling at US ports (at present, selected offshore areas are excluded from dumping); and a new law on solid wastes (rubbish, in plain man's language). The proposed 'solid wastes' law would cover: sanitary land fill to replace open rubbish dumps; tax credits for re-cycling solid waste materials: and probably grants for garbage treatment. (The $287 billion does include an estimate for new policies for solid wastes, however.)

The biggest single industry affected will be the car industry, which will have to redesign engines (and to some extent, other parts of the car) to meet the clean air requirements now being set. Emission controls on exhaust systems have not proved a success. The American car industry, and to a smaller extent garages and service stations, will have to spend some $58 billion over the 10 years. This will add about $350 (or over 10%) to the cost of an average passenger car.

This is not likely to cause great distress in the car industry. In some cases, however, owing to the structure of the industry, problems of local unemployment are expected to arise. This may happen with pulp and paper, where anti-pollution costs are relatively high (from 3½% to 10% in terms of product price increases) and fruit and vegetable canning, where they are low (1.4% to 2.3%). In both cases, though, problems will arise because there are a large number of marginal firms in areas where there is no great abundance of alternative employment.

The prospect is enough to be giving senior Administration officials cause for doubts about the priorities implied in environmental policy. There has been no systematic cost-benefit analysis of the policy at all. But it is realised that most of the benefit from keeping waterways cool and clean is for recreation — and mostly middle-class recreation at that. Water for direct human use can be processed comparatively cheaply. Would it be better to spend some of that $87 billion estimated for water on new schools, for instance? Does it really make sense to spend over half the funds from new environmental programmes on cleaner air?

Such questions are now being asked at least. The priorities of environmental policy in the US are up for a fundamental rethink.

America has come closer than most countries to the ideal of free enterprise for much of its history, and the neglect of social considerations is seen most clearly in its record on pollution.

In many different areas firms have manufactured goods and provided services in a way that reduced their costs of production to a minimum. The pressure of competition has been strong, and the most efficient firm could expect to earn the greatest profit. Private values set the patterns of production and consumption, and ensured that the economy worked in a cost-efficient way. But what of the welfare of society in general?

Farmers have used pesticides as they wished, without undue concern about their side-effects. Aircraft manufacturers have designed engines that would be cheap to produce and to operate, without worrying about their noise level. All have disposed of waste in open rubbish dumps. One man's meat has become another man's poison. The welfare of society has been reduced by the addition of social costs, and the neglect of social benefits. Until, that is, America went 'crazy over its environment'.

The effects of government intervention

Government was given the task of making individuals aware of their social responsibilities. In part this could be achieved by education and voluntary assistance. Most often, however, it would be encouraged either by taxes, or by controls which over-rule market forces. Together these policies should ensure that individuals take both social and private effects into account in future decision making.

The cost of an anti-social act will now be measured in its private cost plus the additional tax or fine it incurs. Where the costs of production were previously quite low, as for instance with the dumping of waste in open tips, they will now be greater because of the social cost that must also be paid for — the cost of covering the tip over once more. The effect on each firm is illustrated in Diagram 1. A price-setting, profit-maximising firm could produce output q_1 and price p_1 on the basis of purely private costs and returns. The addition of a tax, or of costs needed to meet controls, would raise production costs, and shift output and price to q_2 and p_2.

But these policies can only ensure that no further pollution occurs in future. What of the pollution that has accumulated over the past? The 'cost of cleaning up America' must include payments made to restore the environment to its original condition. These payments will be made by government, who must finance them from taxation. On the principle that 'the

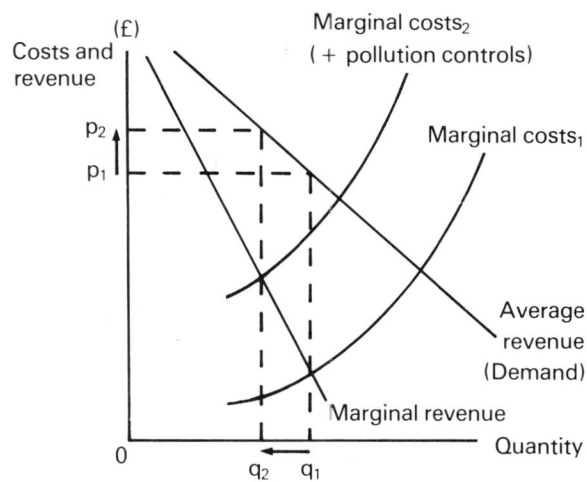

Diagram 1   The cost of pollution controls

polluter must pay', this taxation will fall most heavily on those industries whose record has been particularly unsatisfactory in the past, but it is still a burden that must be shared.

Value for money

The total cost of these environmental programmes is immense. Up to 2.2% of gross national product will be devoted to the improvements described, at a loss in material terms of the cars and other finished products that can no longer be bought.

There will be benefits to society from this spending, but the 'questions now being asked' are whether greater benefits could be gained some other way. Social costs and benefits are difficult to measure, and difficult to compare with the private values that are reflected in free market forces. Only through such a comparison, however, can society match resources to wants in a satisfactory way.

QUESTIONS

(i)   (a) What social benefits might result from 'trim trails'? (b) What social costs might result from 'legalising cannabis'?
(ii)   The criminal law allows the state to claim against individuals, while civil law allows individuals to claim against other individuals. Explain why there is a place for both in preventing pollution.
(iii)   Suggest an explanation of why a 10% rise in costs might cause unemployment in the 'paper and pulp industry', but not in the 'car industry'.

4 Taxation

4.1 Taxes and welfare

Why are 'vices' taxed so heavily? There is the social case that certain activities are morally undesirable, and therefore to be discouraged. But there is also an economic argument that considers, in a more objective way, the welfare of consumers as individuals, and as a collective society. Individual consumers choose goods and services that offer the most satisfaction. Smoking, drinking and gambling can all raise the personal level of welfare if chosen in this way. Consumers benefit from their enjoyment of such vices, but at a private cost that measures the alternative forgone.

In many cases, however, their consumption leads to dissatisfaction for other members of society. Taxes can be used to make individual consumers take account of these external effects. Consumers can choose to smoke, but must pay an amount of tax in addition to the original price. Thus, they pay for both private cost, and the cost to society at large, of their actions. The consumer is penalised rather than discouraged, and the welfare of society is protected.

'When taxes are good for your health'

A social cost results from 'not wearing seat belts', or 'smoking cigarettes'. In these and many other cases, society must devote resources to repairing the health of those who are damaged. It must accept a lower level of output due to the fall in the victims' productivity. It must acknowledge the ill-effects, in danger or discomfort, suffered by other members of society. Society can make its collective feelings felt on these matters by raising the cost of individual actions. It can fine those not wearing seat belts, or raise their insurance costs through taxation. It can make smokers pay on each packet of cigarettes they buy, and fine them for smoking in certain places.

A similar argument applies in cases of social benefit. 'Fluoridation of water' can improve dental health, and reduce the costs of the health service. But this is a benefit that individual consumers might not be aware of, or approve of. Water Boards will

When taxes are good for your health

The Government should not shrink from slapping the highest possible taxes it can think of on things that are bad for our health, if only for the purely mercenary reason that people who damage their insides by smoking and excessive eating and drinking, or break their bodies by driving too fast, can cost other taxpayers a great deal of money when they land up in hospital or in the mortuary. . . .

Perhaps the best example to start with is the proposed new law on seat belts. The Department of Health and Social Security estimates that about 14 000 fatal and serious injuries would be averted every year if all drivers and front seat passengers used seat belts at all times.

The current official estimate of the cost of all accidents is £800m; just how much of it would be saved by avoiding 14 000 serious injuries and fatalities depends on your assumptions and your method of accountancy. If each individual (or his surviving relatives) was obliged to pay the full cost of the accident — in police time, crash recovery services, lost production, medical care, ambulances, and the like — there might be less of a case for making seat belts compulsory. As it is, the new law could have the effect of enabling insurance companies (and future Ministers of Health?) to say to those who were infringing the law by not wearing belts, that they would have to pay up. . . .

tend to consider only private issues in the supply of water.

A subsidy could cover the costs of installing fluoridation plants, and allow both private individuals and society to gain their benefits. This could be financed by taxation levied generally, on all who will benefit in society, or particularly on those consuming 'vices'.

There are two difficulties in all this. One is the practical problem of deciding the value of the costs and benefits involved, and setting the levels of taxes and subsidies. The other is an issue that falls outside the field of economics altogether, for the social responsibility of the community can only be gained at the expense of a loss of freedom on the part of the individual.

Equity

Any tax makes the individual paying it worse off. In cases of social cost this is desirable. In general it is an unfortunate result of the government's wish, part economic, part social and part political, to spend

The cash-benefit principle does not get us around every dispute. One of the preventive measures proposed in the recent Consultative Document is fluoridation of water, and the Government is providing £0.5m towards the small capital costs involved. Water Boards are still proving slow to accept the hint, in spite of the extensive evidence of the benefit in reducing dental decay. The apparently waning anti-fluoride lobby has long based its main argument on the infringement of liberty involved in 'enforced medication' — and it would hardly be practical to propose a differential tariff for householders piped into a special fluoride-free water supply.

But in most cases the money talks, or could if the Government had the courage to pursue the possibility to the limits of public acceptance. . . .

On cigarettes it acknowledges that opinion polls suggest that a majority of people in this country would favour stricter controls — yet the forthcoming draft Order under the Medicines Act will leave the regulation of tobacco (as opposed to substitutes) to voluntary agreement. . . . What has not been properly tried is a higher tax.

The same applies to the drink industry. *Prevention and Health* says there may be 500 000 people with a 'serious drink problem' in England and Wales and proportionately more in Scotland. It puts drink and tobacco in a category by comparison with which 'narcotic addiction is numerically a relatively minor problem.'

to each individual's ability to pay. In this way, the government can raise its revenue, and still protect the general welfare of the community.

Fair taxation

The general welfare of the country and that of every individual rests mainly on the basis, that the burdens of the State shall be borne equally and at the same rate. All authorities, subjects and inhabitants without exception shall contribute in such measure as corresponds to their fortune, condition and income. . . . But in Pomerania there were many poor people, and poor land, especially near Friedland, Hammerstein, Tuchel and on to Konitz. A *pro rata* would have to be worked out; e.g. a rich man with an income of 5000 Thaler could be made to pay 2500, and would still have enough left to live on; but a poor man, with an income of 80 Thaler, could not pay one half, for then he could not live; for him it would be sufficient to pay one out of 80 Thaler.

QUESTIONS

(i) How can a tax on alcoholic drinks affect the welfare of society?

(ii) Explain whether you would expect a tax on cigarettes to be equitable.

(iii) A poor man earns £80 and pays £1 in tax. How much would a man earning £5000 pay if tax rates were (a) proportional, (b) regressive?

---

revenue. How is the burden to be shared?

Equity requires that taxes should be the same for taxpayers in the same circumstances, paid at a convenient time, and set in a fair and open way. Above all they should be related to each taxpayer's ability to pay. Generally it is agreed that higher incomes should be taxed more heavily, and that a certain level of income should not be taxed at all. Every individual should receive the necessities of life without having to pay tax. This is achieved through progressive tax rates, which raise the tax bill more than proportionately to a rise in income.

'Fair taxation'

This principle has been accepted since at least the eighteenth century. Frederick the Great thought that a rich man should pay half his income in tax, but for a poor man, 'it would be sufficient to pay one out of 80'. This is highly progressive taxation, perhaps more progressive than would be acceptable in view of the distribution of income today. It results in 'the burdens of the State being borne equally' in relation

4.2 Taxes and efficiency

'Tax cuts and tax revenue'

Taxes raise revenue for the government to finance its spending. To do so efficiently they must raise as much revenue as possible for the least administrative cost. The tax system that can achieve this most successfully will be simple rather than complicated,

---

Tax cuts and tax revenue

Perhaps the best method of giving a summary view of the case will be by my stating to the Committee what will be the financial results of the treaty as it stands. I will not enter into any of the smaller details, and will take three branches of reduction only – the reduction of the duty upon wine, the reduction of that upon brandy, and the abolition of the duties upon manufactured goods. The reduction of the duty upon wine from 5s 10d to 3s per gallon will afford to the consumer a relief of £830 000, and will entail upon the revenue, after allowing for an increase of consumption to the extent of 35 per cent, a loss of £515 000. The reduction of the duty upon brandy from 15s to 8s 2d a gallon will give to the consumer a relief of £446 000, and, assuming that the consumption will be raised to the point at which it stood in 1850, just before the disease of the vine commenced, it will cause a loss of £225 000 to the revenue. . . .

---

and rely on a few taxes which each raise a great deal in revenue.

Each tax will be set at a certain rate, which determines the level of revenue that can be raised. Raising that rate may increase or decrease tax revenue, depending on elasticity. The government will find it easiest to raise revenue from taxes on goods in inelastic demand, and on factors in inelastic supply.

This was the problem faced by Gladstone, as Chancellor of the Exchequer, when predicting the effects of tax cuts in 1860. He expected, for example, that a fall in the duty on wine, from 5s 10d to 3s a gallon would involve a loss of tax revenue of £515 000. Demand would respond little to the fall in price, as it was relatively inelastic.

If demand rose much more than he expected, however, the effect on tax revenue would not be so severe. Suppose that consumers bought an extra 3 433 333 gallons because of the fall in tax and price of wine. This would yield an extra (3 433 333 × 3s =) £515 000 to the Chancellor, and the tax revenue would not fall at all.

This is one case where it was expected that a tax

could raise revenue most effectively by being set at higher rates. The overall structure of taxation would need to take this into account, and the revenue-earning powers of all other taxes in the same way, if it were to operate efficiently.

The supply of factors

But taxation can affect efficiency in more far-reaching ways than this. Anything that is taxed is, to some extent, discouraged, and an unbalanced system of taxation will discourage some things more than others. Taxes that fall directly upon the income of factors of production can have a disincentive effect that will result in reduced employment and output. Taxes that fall only on particular goods and services will discourage their consumption, and affect the way resources are directed towards the satisfaction of consumer wants. Some of these effects may be intended, but others will be unintentional. The inefficiency that results will be a cost of following other aims of taxation.

A tax can be levied directly on either the supply or demand of products or factors. In any case there will be a change in market conditions, and it is this that can bring a disincentive effect. A lump-sum tax per unit paid by suppliers, for instance, will raise the price at which each quantity can be offered to the market. Unless demand or supply are perfectly

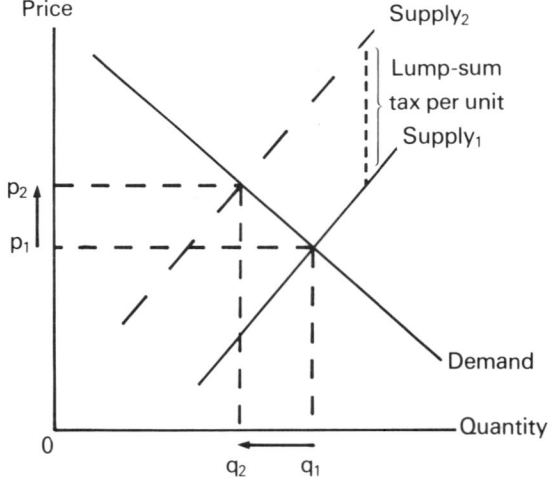

Diagram 1   A tax on supply

inelastic, this will bring a fall in equilibrium quantity in the market (Diagram 1). In the next section we will consider the effect on price.

Where the tax falls on the supply of a factor, it is possible for two quite opposite effects to follow. On the one hand, the fall in the factor's earnings will encourage it to transfer out of the market, to any alternative that exists. This follows whenever transfer earnings are taxed, supply slopes 'normally', and is less than totally inelastic. On the other hand, the owners of the factors may try to maintain their income whatever the rate of pay. There is no alternative they prefer, and their supply is 'backward' sloping. They will offer to work more if the taxman cuts their pay, and less if he increases it. Which effect applies in practice?

'Taxation and incentives in the UK'

Income tax falls on the supply of labour, employers' surcharges fall on the demand for labour, and national insurance contributions affect both. Corporation tax falls on the return from capital, and investment grants and allowances subsidise it. There is evidence that both labour and capital respond to the incentive whenever these taxes are reduced.

In the case of labour, it appears that a 'reduction of the basic rate of tax from 33% to 30% would initially increase supply by about 0.6%'. The supply of labour is 'indeed upward sloping'. In the case of capital there is a similar response to corporation tax, although it is much stronger in the services sector than in the manufacturing sector of the economy. Supply, again, is upward sloping.

If this is true, then there is a case for saying that 'we need incentives', and should reduce the burden of taxation on the income of factors.

Taxation and incentives in the UK

'We need to strengthen incentives, by allowing people to keep more of what they earn . . .' Sir Geoffrey Howe, Budget Speech, 12 June 1979

Much of the argument about the effects of taxation on the supply of labour revolves around the question of whether the supply schedule of labour is upward sloping, i.e. higher wage rates generate more labour supply. If this condition is satisfied it follows that taxation which reduces the disposable real wage will result in a lower supply of labour. Some recent estimates[1] suggest that the labour supply schedule is indeed upward sloping with an elasticity of about 0.1. On this basis the reduction of the basic rate of tax from 33 per cent to 30 per cent would initially increase the supply of labour by about 0.6 per cent.

In the same study it was found that taxation also affects the demand for labour by firms. In particular, various employment surcharges such as SET, employers' national insurance contributions, etc. have the effect of reducing labour demand and employment. A one per cent rise in these surcharges eventually has the effect of reducing employment by about 1.4 per cent. It would therefore seem that, in a variety of ways, UK employment is sensitive to taxation.

In another study[2] it has been shown that investment in the distributive and services sector is sensitive to the rate of corporation tax and investment grants and allowances. This study suggests that if, for example, corporation tax were to fall from 52 per cent to 45 per cent, cumulative net investment in the sector would rise by about 7.6 per cent so that output in the sector would eventually rise by about 2.25 per cent. It further suggests if the discounted cash flow from investment grants and allowances were to rise by 10 per cent, cumulative net investment would eventually rise by about 5 per cent. In the manufacturing sector, the latter response is somewhat lower at 3 per cent. On the other hand, manufacturing investment did not seem sensitive to corporation tax, reflecting perhaps the ability of the companies concerned to avoid the payment of mainstream corporation tax.

[1] M Beenstock, 'Does the UK Labour Market Work?' *Economic Outlook*, July 1979.
[2] Carried out by Ruth Kosmin in preparation for her doctoral dissertation.

QUESTIONS

(i)   Why should taxes on cigarettes and alcoholic drinks be efficient at raising revenue for the government?

(ii)   Assume that the labour market is in equilibrium when the government raises the standard rate of income tax from 30% to 33%, and employment surcharges by 1%. Explain the result you would expect in the labour market.

(iii)   Explain how you would expect an increase in indirect taxes, such as VAT, to affect the supply of labour.

(iv)   Suggest two ways in which a reduction in income tax might increase national output.

4.3 The burden of taxation

The government has four main aims to consider in setting its pattern of taxation. In the order in which we have met them, these are:

1 to balance private with social cost,
2 to spread the burden of taxation in an equitable way,
3 to raise revenue as efficiently as possible, with a minimum of administrative cost,
4 to avoid undesirable disincentive effects.

Individual taxes are not likely to meet all of these requirements, but the overall system of taxation should be able to achieve a balance between them. In this way, the government will fulfil its microeconomic obligations towards welfare and efficiency.

But what of its social and political targets? It may well try to adjust the distribution of income within society, and the pattern of behaviour in the economy, for reasons that are all its own. As economists we cannot say what the government should or should not choose to do in these areas; but we can predict the effects of different policies. To do so we must ask where the burden of taxation falls. There is no straightforward answer to this question.

'Business's turn for tax cuts'

At first sight it appears that UK companies have suffered from a heavy and increasing burden, or incidence, of taxation. They must pay Value Added Tax on the value of their business, Corporation tax on the level of their profits, local rates on the value of their property, and national insurance contributions on their employment of labour.

If all of these taxes had to be paid exclusively from the profits of business the burden would be heavy indeed: so heavy that many companies would go out of business, and the government would raise very little in revenue. In practice, of course, much of the burden is passed on to the owners of factors employed by companies, or to the customers who buy their products.

Consider the effect of a lump-sum tax on the sale of a particular good, paid to the taxman by producers. Companies can now afford to sell each quantity of the good only at the original level of price, plus the amount of the tax. This change in the

---

Business's turn for tax cuts

The UK is peculiar in the types of tax that it levies on corporations. The burden of corporation income taxes as a percentage of total tax, in spite of the large number and variety of reliefs, is average compared with most countries apart from Japan and the US. The burden of local authority rates on business is quite exceptionally high, at 5 per cent of all tax revenue. It is far higher than similar property taxes in most other countries, and slightly higher even than in Canada and the United States, the other main countries which use such taxes. The burden of national insurance contributions by employers has been relatively light. But the introduction of the national insurance surcharge in 1977 has brought the UK nearer to the international average.

... Although taxes on corporations have gone up by 90 per cent in current money to £16.8bn between 1976 and 1979, the rise is only 30 per cent in real inflation-adjusted terms. This is still a considerable extra burden over a period when real GDP has gone up by only about 7 per cent. Taxes on corporations rose from a low point of 19 per cent of all taxes in 1975 and 1976 to 26½ per cent of all taxes in 1979.... National insurance taxes have roughly held their share. Corporation tax has also held its share, but with an important switch from advance to mainstream tax as retained profits have risen in relation to distributions. The share of rates has dropped, while that of North Sea oil and gas taxes has risen from virtually nothing to nearly 7 per cent.

Tax incidence

The figures given could be challenged on the grounds that some of the taxes included fall in reality not on corporations but on consumers, since they are passed on in prices. This depends on the complex theory of tax incidence − on whom taxes ultimately fall, rather than by whom they are paid in the first place − which is even more subject to disagreement than most branches of economics. It can be argued that all taxes on business, even corporation tax, are passed on in higher prices, leaving corporations with nil tax incidence; or on the other hand that rates and national insurance contributions − and even expenditure taxes such as VAT − fall at least in part on the factors of production − land, labour and capital; corporations might then have a tax incidence even higher than the taxes which they themselves pay.

It depends on such matters as demand for the product, union bargaining power, the degree of competition, and so on. It seems simpler to begin by taking the taxes actually paid by corporations as a first approximation − remembering that some taxes such as VAT and PAYE, while paid by consumers, are collected and passed on by corporations. The importance of theories of tax incidence is that they may offer some guide to the effects of a cut or an increase in any particular tax at a specific point in the business cycle.

conditions of supply leads to excess demand for the good at the original price level, and encourages a change in market price and quantity.

In most cases there will be a fall in the quantity bought and sold, and a rise in price. The fall in quantity follows the disincentive effect described in the last section. The rise in price determines the burden of taxation on buyers and sellers respectively.

At one extreme, the price might rise by the full amount of the tax. Consumers will pay all of the tax levied on each unit traded, while producers need to pay none. At the other extreme, price might not rise at all. Consumers will pay none of the tax, so producers must absorb all of the cost internally.

Elasticities of demand and supply

The burden of indirect taxation borne by buyers and sellers is decided by their respective elasticities of demand and supply.

This burden can be seen in terms of the total tax revenue taken from each group in the market, where total revenue is the product of price and quantity. In Diagram 1, the burden falls almost equally on

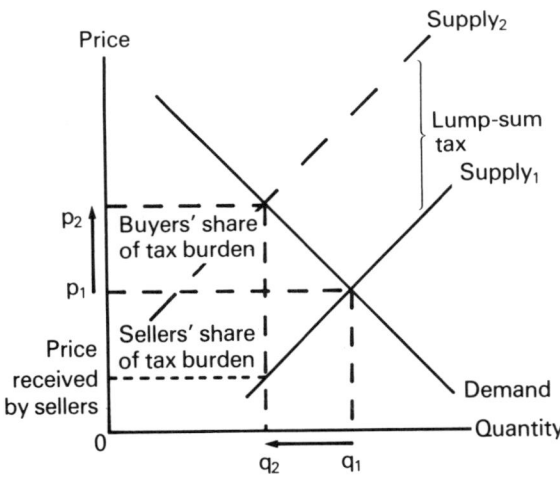

Total tax revenue = buyers' share + sellers' share

Diagram 1   The burden of taxation

producers and consumers, such are the relative elasticities of supply and demand.

Companies in the UK face very different market conditions for both their products and their factors. For some elasticities are high, for others they are low. Tax rates do not discriminate, and the burden of taxation falls rather unequally between different companies as a result.

How will a company be best protected from the effects of taxation? First it requires the 'demand for the product' to be inelastic, which is helped by keeping the 'degree of competition' very low. Next it must be willing and able to transfer into an alternative line of business, in order to keep its own price elasticity of supply very high. In these circumstances it may hope that 'all taxes on business . . . are passed on in higher prices'.

All this is in the product market. In its factor market the company must hope that its market situation is reversed. Its demand for factors must be highly elastic, which requires that the firm can substitute one for another quickly and easily. The supply of factors must be highly inelastic, so that factor earnings are mostly economic rent. In the case of labour, it will be important, on both counts, that 'union bargaining power' is weak.

Few companies can meet these requirements. Market forces provide them with no escape from the burden of taxation. For that they must rely on their accountants instead, or wait till it is 'Business's turn for tax cuts'.

QUESTIONS

(i)   Explain how you would expect the burden of tax on cigarettes to be divided between producers and consumers.

(ii)   How successful would you expect a tax on the profits from North Sea oil production (*not* exploration) to be, in terms of the government's aims of taxation?

(iii)   What reason(s) are there for making necessity goods exempt from Value Added Tax?

(iv)   Explain how a profit-maximising entrepreneur will decide when it is time for him to close his business under the burden of taxation.

5 Stocks

5.1 The problems of agriculture

Governments throughout the world choose to intervene in agriculture. We can explain this special treatment for the industry in terms of three characteristics that apply far and wide to a great variety of crops and livestock. They arise from the part played by primary products in political and strategic issues, from the unusual conditions of supply and demand in primary markets, and from the cyclical nature of market behaviour over periods of time.

We will study these issues one at a time; together they make a strong and general case for intervention by government in agricultural markets. This will allow us to move on, in the next section, from the reasons for intervention to the methods that are used.

The strategic role of agriculture

Food is a basic requirement for life. A similar priority is given to many of the other raw materials that are the products of agriculture. It is important, therefore, that a country should command some measure of self-sufficiency in the production of these commodities. It will then be able to preserve its independence and security in world affairs, and bargain from a position of strength in time of war or of trade sanctions.

These are political considerations, but they can be justified by a government if they raise the economic welfare of a country's citizens, at least over the long term. The decision to support agricultural production at home, however, may involve no little cost. Other countries will often be more efficient at producing primary products, and resources could be used more profitably at home in the production of different goods and services.

Nevertheless, the UK has followed the path of agricultural support for many years and in company with many other countries. She has never come close to being self-sufficient, but has always been able to make up the balance of supplies from secure political allies such as the Commonwealth, and the European Economic Community.

'Farm Policy'

Governments within the EEC intervene in support of agriculture under the terms of the Common Agricultural Policy. This policy has many objectives, some of which are political, and some economic. It has achieved 'stable prices' and a 'long-term framework' for the industry. It has led, however, to many disagreements among members of the Community.

But in perhaps the most important way, the policy has 'served Europe well'. It has gone a large part of the way towards strategic self-sufficiency in agricultural production. It has given Europe 'secure supplies of food'.

Conditions of supply and demand

The production of primary products depends on the weather and other natural conditions. This is different from the production of most manufactured goods, and results in frequent changes in the supply of crops and livestock. Output is difficult to predict, and there are many fluctuations in market price and quantity.

Whenever there is a shift in supply or demand, the change in price required to clear the market is relatively great. Both supply and demand tend to be highly inelastic with respect to price. Supply is restricted by natural forces over given periods of time. Crops take time to grow and livestock takes time to be reared for market. Demand also responds little to price changes, since consumers see agricultural products as necessities for life and cannot replace them by other goods.

These market conditions result in major changes in the distribution of income between producers and consumers. The total revenue paid for agricultural goods is the product of their price and their output. What is paid out by consumers, is received as income by producers. Frequent changes in supply, and large price adjustments due to low elasticities, cause that sum to fluctuate greatly to the benefit of first one group, and then the other.

'Every cloud has a silver lining'

Good weather conditions have brought 'bumper harvests' of cereals, potatoes and apples. Farmers have 'never had better yields' and their supply to the market has increased greatly. So what do they have 'to moan about'?

'High production leads to low prices.' Inelastic demand and supply mean that the original excess

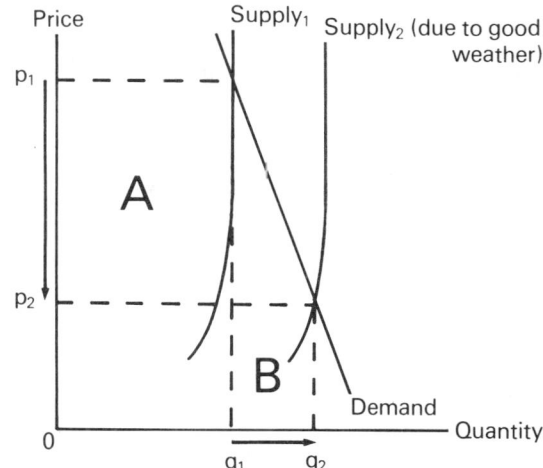

Total revenue = price × quantity. Farmers lose revenue A, and gain revenue B due to good weather.

Diagram 1   Market conditions in agriculture

of supply can only be cleared by more than proportionate reductions in price. Farmers gain from their increased sales, but lose even more due to lower prices (Diagram 1). The total revenue earned by farmers and paid by consumers falls as a result. The distribution of income moves against farmers and in favour of consumers. This is 'the cloud' that hangs over farmers, but the 'silver lining that shoppers are waiting for'.

Production and price cycles

Agricultural markets that are left to their own devices tend to suffer from continuing cycles of production and price changes. The high farm production and low prices that were caused by good weather would probably be followed by low production and high prices, then high production and low prices once more, and so on.

The theoretical explanation of this behaviour is based on two conditions: that future production is planned on the basis of present prices, and that there is a delay between planning production and achieving it. An initial shift of supply will then set up continuing fluctuations in the market that only the co-ordination of producers, or the intervention of government, can overcome.

'The pig cycle'

There was a marked cycle in both the production and prices of pigs in Ireland between the wars. A low number of pigs were marketed in one year, which caused their price to rise. This encouraged farmers to

---

Every cloud has a silver lining

People not closely in touch with Britain's farmlands are inclined to think we have had a poor summer. There were a lot of clouds and a lot of rain seemed to fall from them. But the country is full of happy farmers getting in the last rich instalments of bumper harvests.... Reports from all over Britain tell of bulging storage silos and confirm the official forecasts that the cereal harvest could be a record 17½ million tons – up by more than half a million tons on last year. The weather began preparing the golden news last year. A good dry autumn enabled far more of the heavier yielding winter wheat than usual to be sown. The wet summer has provided almost ideal conditions for plant growth. A reprieve, with long spells of sunshine in many areas from mid-August onwards, allowed the grain to fill and ripen.

Southern farmers such as Giles Rowsell, whose family grows more than 1000 acres of cereals near Winchester, were most favoured. He says: 'We have never had better yields and I can't think that we will ever be so lucky again.'

For once, then, do farmers have little to moan about? That would be too much to expect. All the farmers questioned were quick to point out that high production usually leads to low prices. The cereal harvest in the whole northern hemisphere has been so good that farmers cannot expect to receive more than the acceptable but low EEC guaranteed prices.

So many good-quality potatoes are flooding on to the market that the price to farmers has fallen to 1½p per pound. 'We need at least 2½p to make a reasonable commercial profit,' says Frank Arden.

Fine apples are weighing down the trees in Worcestershire, Kent and Sussex. A colleague was offered as many as she liked free to feed her horse. Hens, too, appear to be more prolific than ever. Giles Rowsell says there is such an egg glut that he is getting only 28p a dozen for the fine brown eggs his 40 000 flock produces. 'That's 10p per dozen below the cost of production,' he says, 'but I have seen no sign of egg prices dropping in the shops.'

That is the silver lining that shoppers are waiting for.

begin rearing more stock in order to increase supply to the market, when those pigs were grown, two years later. This rise in supply, however, only served to depress prices, so reducing planned production for the next two years.

Both price and quantity rose and fell, about every two years (see Table 1). In 1928, for example, the price of pigs was only about £2.50 per hundredweight liveweight. In 1930, farmers offered only 315 000 pigs for sale, and price rose to £3.15. As a result, production rose in 1932 to 370 000, and price fell to £2.25. Only 290 000 pigs were marketed in 1934.

Table 1   The pig cycle in Ireland

Year	1926	28	30	32	34	36	38
Quantity (000 pigs marketed)	215	380	315	385	290	350	280
Price (Moving average, in £ per cwt. l.w.)	3.15	2.50	3.10	2.25	3.25	2.90	3.05

Farmers had no other guidelines or support to help them, and continued the 'cobweb' cycle of fluctuations over this six-year period. It is unlikely that market conditions remained unchanged, and in Diagram 2 it is implied that demand shifted to a modest extent at one stage. The changes in price and output, however, are due much more to the natural instability of the market in its response to price, than to a change in any particular condition of demand or supply.

QUESTIONS

(i)   Explain the conditions under which a good harvest would raise farmers' incomes.

(ii)   Refer to Diagram 2. If the government wished to stabilise the market price, (a) what level of price should it try to maintain in the long term? (b) In order to do so, how many pigs should have been bought by the authorities in 1928, and (c) sold in 1930?

(iii)   Explain how the cobweb cycle would be affected if (a) we considered cattle, which take five years to rear for market, rather than pigs, (b) farmers could co-ordinate their plans for production.

(iv)   Estimate elasticities ($\frac{\% \text{ change in quantity}}{\% \text{ change in price}}$) in 'the pig cycle' from 1928-30, for (a) the price elasticity of demand, (b) the price elasticity of supply in the long-term, (c) the price elasticity of supply in any given year.

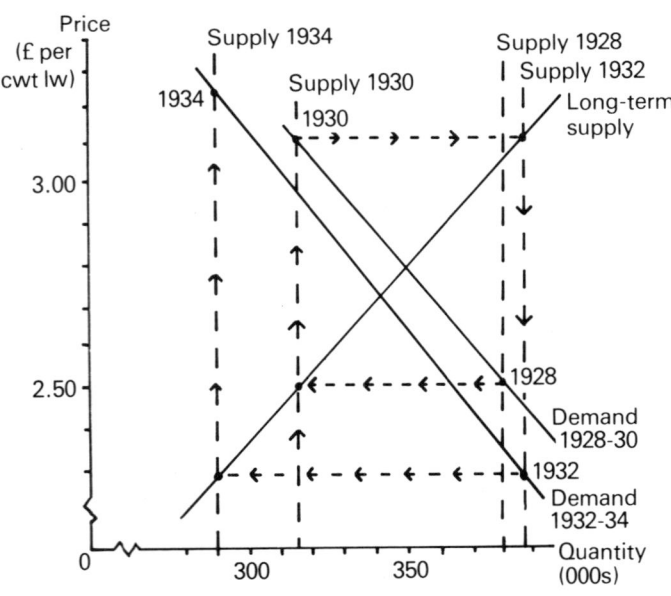

Diagram 2

5.2 Buffer stocks

Agriculture suffers from fluctuations in production and price that change the distribution of income and unsettle production plans. Governments intervene to introduce stability to the market, to maintain a secure level of output, and to influence the incomes of producers and consumers. There are many ways in which they can choose to intervene, and there are techniques suited to many other markets as well as agriculture. The one method we will study here is for governments to buy and sell on their own behalf in the market, holding stocks as a buffer to allow them to do so.

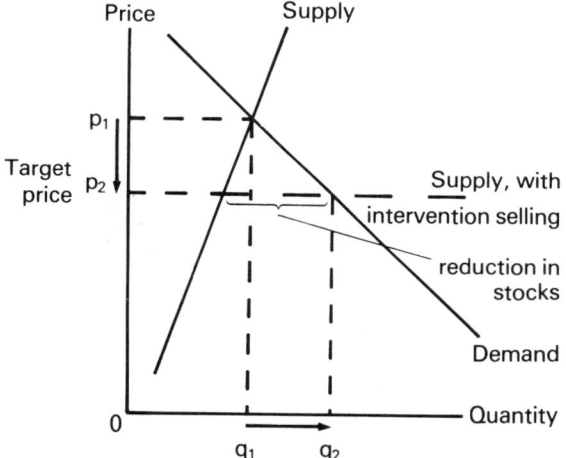

Diagram 1 Intervention selling

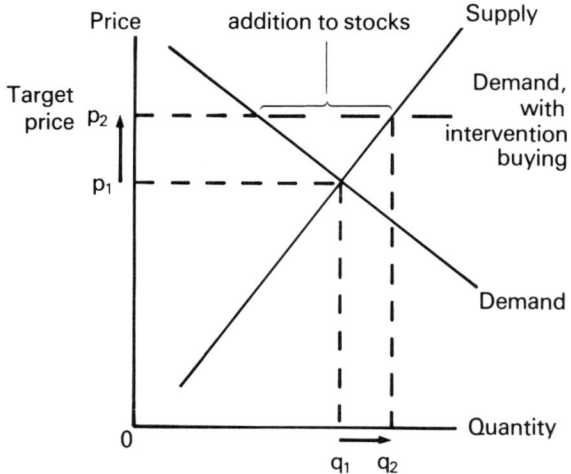

Diagram 2 Intervention buying

The authorities must first decide the level of price which they wish to maintain. This could be that which will clear the market, matching supply to demand in the long term. Alternatively it could be set higher to encourage greater production, and to protect farmers' incomes.

Price will tend to rise above this target, however it is set, when there is a shortage in the market. The authorities will need to increase supply to the market by releasing some of their stocks (see Diagram 1). Price will tend to fall when there is a glut, and the authorities will buy in the market, adding to their stocks (Diagram 2). In either case, they can expect to maintain their desired price.

If all goes well there will be a fall in stocks one year and a rise the next. Stocks will tend to balance over a period and provide a buffer against natural fluctuations in supply. Producers will benefit from stable prices, and consumers from secure supplies.

'Why coffee will never be cheap again'

Brazil supplies a 'third of world trade' in coffee, and suffers from time to time from large fluctuations in production and price. Severe frosts can damage the harvest of coffee beans and reduce output as much as from '28 million bags to only 6 million'. As a result, price changes from below £3000 a ton to above £4000 in a period as short as from one harvest to the next. The impact of this on the incomes of those in the trade and on the balance of payments is most severe, but can be offset by buffer stocks.

The authorities held large stocks of coffee before the frosts, amounting to as much as '65 million bags 10 years ago'. A series of market shortages caused them to release stock on to the market, keeping price relatively stable (at P_2 in Diagram 1). Unfortunately there was no period of surplus during which stocks could recover, before the frosts came. As a result, 'the stockpile was now almost finished' at 1.2 million bags.

Intervention selling could not hide the shortage caused by the frosts, and market price rose to clear the market (to P_1 in Diagram 1). Buyers were discouraged, and there was a '20% drop in coffee consumption in the UK'.

Intervention buying

The concern of coffee producers now is to rebuild their stocks. They will hope for good harvests and a surplus of production to allow them to do so. This will 'steer the industry into a position where coffee prices will stabilise' in the years ahead.

But what of the consumers? They have been faced

27

Brazilians explain why coffee will never be cheap again

There is not an awful lot of coffee in Brazil at the moment – a mere 1.2 million bags in reserve at the end of last month, in a fast-diminishing stockpile. . . .

Dr Calazans, a 48-year-old banker with an imposing figure befitting the most powerful man in the trade, said the freak frost of two years ago, which all but decimated the Brazilian plantations, was the main single fact why coffee has soared from about 40p retail for a 4oz jar to a peak of £1.50.

The frost, he said, destroyed more than half of Brazil's 2.8 billion trees at a time when the country controlled a massive third of world trade. He told me that 'the frosts come about every three years and we are due for another.'

'The harvest previous to the frost produced 28 million bags. In 1976, it amounted to only 6 million bags, which meant digging into our already dwindling stockpile.' At 1.2m bags, against 65m 10 years ago, the stockpile was now almost finished.

The recent agreement to build up stockpiles as a cushion against both demand and weather hazards, thrashed out by Latin-American producing nations in Mexico last month, was not an attempt to corner the market. 'It is an international agreement designed to steer the industry into a position where coffee prices will stabilise,' he said. . . .

Although the doctor did not mention it in his address, he told me his Government's policy was to see prices settle around $3 a pound on the world market. That is somewhere near the present level of £2770 a metric ton and way below the peak of £4200.

Leonard Adams, director of Brooke-Bond Liebig's coffee division and one of the British delegates, said: 'I am surprised he quoted $3. It would be very nice if the coffee prices stabilised at around £1.50 a pound. At the peak, we were paying about £4.50. I think it would be possible to retail a 4oz jar for about 75p – which is a lot less than today's prices. . . .

'What we have to do is stabilise prices. There is nothing worse than uncertainty. You get prices of £4000 a ton one day in London and then in a very short time you are trading at £3000 a ton. You don't want too much coffee in stock with that going on. Because everyone is uncertain at the moment, no one is holding very much stock in the pipeline.'

The recent price spiral has meant a 20% drop in coffee consumption in the UK, and that is serious for the industry, which will now be awaiting the results of a meeting in London this week when the International Coffee Organisation discusses stockpiling. The redoubtable Dr Calazans will be there to put Brazil's case.

---

with higher prices due to the frosts. They are now to be faced with continuing high prices due to the intervention buying of stockholders. 'Coffee will never be cheap again' – at least not until, in the very long term, the buffer stock system can work once more on a year-to-year basis.

Stocks can be held by individuals in the market whether they are producers, dealers, or even consumers. The 'uncertainty', and the cost of doing so, however, make this a function more suited to the work of collective organisations, or of governments. An 'agreement . . . by Latin-American producing nations' is a step in this direction, by those most directly involved in the market for coffee.

If their intervention fails to work well, both the market and the authorities will suffer. The market will again be afflicted by fluctuations, and insecurity, and the authorities will acquire either a shortage or a surplus of stocks.

Even if intervention does work well, there will be costs for the authorities to bear. First there is the cost of storage which, for bulky and perishable produce, will be high. Then there is the cost of acquiring stock, and of holding on to produce that could bring satisfaction in consumption. Finally there may be a cost in disposing of stocks that move too far into surplus.

'Market set to sell off surplus wine to Russians'

The Common Agricultural Policy has led to surplus stocks of many commodities. The EEC has acquired 'wine lakes' and 'butter and dried milk mountains' of remarkable proportions: 60 million gallons of wine, £500 million worth of dairy goods, and a million tons of dried milk. In addition to the costs of acquiring and witholding so much produce, there must be major costs of storage. How have these surpluses come about, and how can they be disposed of?

Any system of intervention dealing requires the authorities to estimate market forces in advance, and to choose which level of price they wish to maintain. Their prediction may prove to be inaccurate. Supply can be affected by weather conditions, by technical improvements, and by the tastes of farmers. Demand can be changed by relative prices, incomes, or tastes. The authorities may set their target price above that implied by long-term supply and demand alone. They

Market set to sell off surplus wine to Russians

The Common Market is ready to subsidise the export of surplus French and Italian wine to the Soviet Union, in the same way that butter was sold to the Russians two years ago. . . .

The Russian sale will help syphon off the Community's 'wine lake,' the product of two bumper harvests and a permanent excess of production over consumption. With 60 million gallons likely to be exported, the cost of the subsidy could be more than £8½ million. . . .

It is the EEC's guaranteed price system that has led to the 'wine lake,' stimulating a steady growth in production, which was helped by record-breaking harvests. . . . Consumption has failed to keep pace, especially in France, where campaigns against alcoholism and rising popularity of other drinks have reduced demand for the traditional *vin ordinaire*. . . . A wine surplus is likely to be a feature of Market economy for many years, and Pierre Lardinois, who is in charge of the Common Agricultural Policy, expects sales to the Soviet Union to become a regular operation.

Subsidising exports is in fact a far cheaper way of disposing of surplus plonk than the main alternative, which is distilling it. . . .

Despite the political implications of the forthcoming deal, Brussels experts point out that it is a drop in the bucket compared with the cost of getting rid of other surpluses. With a dried milk mountain of up to a million tons looming over them, and dairy sector support scheduled to cost £500 million, . . . worried Eurocrats can be forgiven for tending to see the wine export deal as light relief.

may wish to encourage production, or to bolster farmers' incomes for political reasons.

When these possibilities all combine, the result is a surplus of stocks bought in by the authorities. This is the situation that has applied to the operation of the Common Agricultural Policy, and has raised the problem of how to dispose of surplus 'wine lakes'.

Any stocks released on the European market will depress prices below the level taken by the authorities as their target. They must dispose of the surplus in a way that prevents this possibility. In the case of wine, distilling into industrial alcohol would be an acceptable, but expensive solution. It is cheaper and just as effective to sell the surplus, at a subsidised price, to the Soviet Union.

Even so, there will be a cost in disposing of surplus stocks of wine, and of other agricultural products. The Russian sale will cost the EEC 'more than £8½ million' in export subsidies, and who knows how much in political terms.

QUESTIONS

(i) Refer to 'Every cloud has a silver lining' on page 25. What measures were used by the EEC to protect farmers? What effect did they have on farmers and stocks?

(ii) How would you estimate the cost of carrying stocks of coffee at their level 'of 10 years ago'?

(iii) What would be the result of a successful attempt by a profit-maximiser to 'corner the market' in coffee?

(iv) Explain, and illustrate with a supply and demand diagram of the EEC market for wine before government intervention, how the surplus has come about.

6 Public ownership

6.1 State enterprise

'The biggest boss in Britain'

The state has many ways of influencing the market economy, but perhaps the most far-reaching is through the public ownership of trading organisations. State enterprise can take different forms, including trade by central and local government, and whole- or part-nationalisation of industry. Public enterprise also meets many buyers and sellers in the private sector in the course of its everyday trade.

The British government has become 'the biggest boss in Britain'. The departments of central and local government do not always trade a marketed product, but the nationalised industries do. These have been taken into full state ownership, and trade in goods and services that are basic to the economy. There are also many companies in which the state has taken a measure of ownership. The scope of this ownership changed greatly after the introduction of the National Enterprise Board.

The scale of state enterprise in itself affects the performance of the economy. The motivation, efficiency and social responsibility of business is different in the public and private sectors. The concentration of industry into larger and less competitive units is encouraged.

The state commands a dominant position over the economy in terms of output, employment and investment. There is scarcely any market that it is unable to affect in a direct or indirect way. Britain is still far short of being fully controlled and planned by the state, but the behaviour of the public sector is crucial to the economy.

QUESTIONS

(i)   How do 'public servants' and 'cigar-smoking financiers' differ in motivation?

(ii)   What is the significance of the difference in the state's share-holding in Fairey, Ferranti and ICL in the extract?

(iii)   The state owns shares, and 'lays out further subsidies' to British Leyland. Compare the effects of each form of support.

The biggest boss in Britain

The most important employer and the biggest spender in this country is the State.

Decisions which affect the jobs and the livelihoods of millions are taken not in the carpeted boardrooms of cigar-smoking financiers, but in the carpeted boardrooms of public servants and Government appointees.

Almost one worker in three has his wages paid by the Government.

There are 7 314 000 people directly employed by Whitehall departments, local councils and public corporations compared with 17 447 000 in the private sector.

But the State's influence and control over the supposedly private enterprise section of the economy is also growing endlessly.

The National Enterprise Board, darling of Tony Benn and favourite off-spring of the Labour Party National Executive, now has big stakes in almost 40 companies.

Some of them are household names, firms which the man in the street would often assume to be anything but nationalised.

Most people know British Leyland is State run. The NEB's 95 per cent shareholding cost the taxpayer £246 million, and huge sums are being laid out in further subsidies.

But consider this further selection from the NEB basket:

Fairey Engineering: 100% – cost £18 million.
Ferranti: 50% – cost £6 million.
Herbert: 100% – cost £26 million.
ICL: 24.4% – cost £12 million.
Rolls-Royce: 100% – cost £196 million.

But that is only the National Enterprise Board package.

There are many more concerns, some successful, some not, in which the Government now holds large or controlling interests.

With every year and every Budget, with every Act of Parliament and every new Government policy, the grip of the State on British industry and commerce grows tighter.

6.2 Nationalisation

A firm is nationalised when its shares are taken into public ownership. An industry is nationalised so that the state can take over all, or most, of the firms producing certain goods or services, and it does so for political or economic ends. The political issues may carry more weight in some areas, but the economic arguments are all we shall consider here. They may differ with the particular circumstances of each industry, but will, in general, concern both the cost efficiency of the industry itself, and the welfare of society as a whole.

Efficiency

When firms are combined into a single organisation it is possible for production to become either more or less efficient. On the one hand, the industry may gain from economies of scale that were not available to individual firms. The cost of producing each unit of output will fall, and allow the industry to pass on this benefit to its customers in lower prices (see Diagram 1).

On the other hand, the industry may lose its motive to reduce costs, and so produce inefficiently. It will face little competition, and need take less care to achieve a least-cost combination of factors at each output level. There will be less pressure to improve products and production techniques. Trade unions may be in a stronger position to command wage rises. There may even be difficulties in administration, and diseconomies of scale.

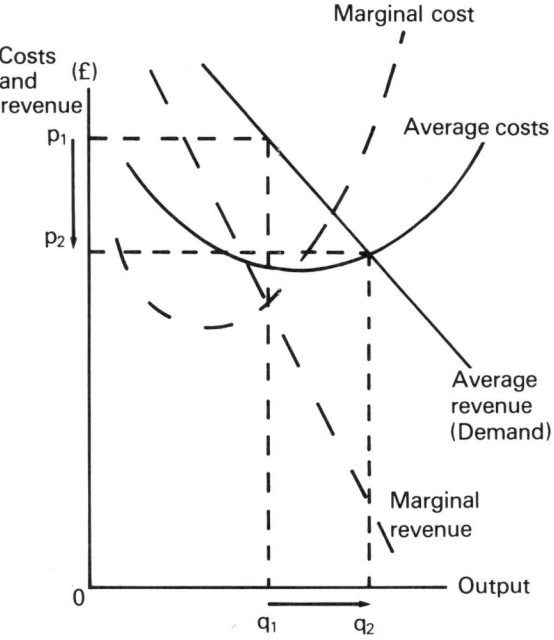

1 = if a private sector firm, profit-maximising
2 = possible policy if nationalised

Diagram 2   Output and price under monopoly

Welfare

Firms in the private sector can take account only of private costs and benefits. This is likely to lead them to be profit-maximising, and to ignore the social results of their actions.

Profit-maximising monopolies can exploit consumers, limit output and raise price (see Diagram 2). State-owned monopolies have very different motives, and can set output and price at levels that best serve the public interest.

Nationalisation of 'natural', entrenched monopolies can change motivation and behaviour in this way, but is likely also to raise the level of concentration in the economy, and the degree of monopoly power in the industry. It will make it possible, however, for production to take account of social costs and benefits. The industries chosen for nationalisation are often those where society has much to gain — communications, power, and basic manufacturing.

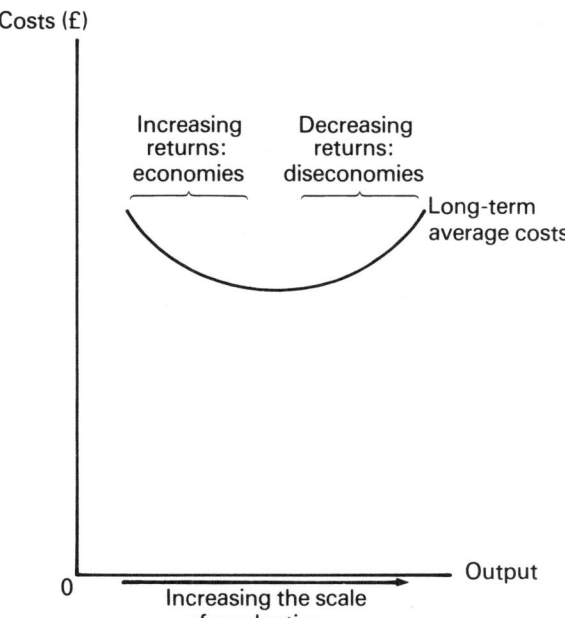

Diagram 1   Returns to scale

'Banking and finance'

Let us consider the proposal that 'the big four private clearing banks be brought into public ownership, together with a merchant bank'. What is the economic case for this act of nationalisation?

There is little that could be gained in terms of efficiency. Each bank is already large and can benefit from most of the economies of scale that are possible in their line of business. This is acknowledged in the proposal that 'the separate identities of Britain's biggest clearing banks should be maintained'. Some co-ordination of policies, and sharing of funds, property and equipment could presumably be arranged. The additional services of a merchant bank would benefit the organisation. But these economies would be relatively modest.

The main part of the case for nationalisation concerns the position of the banks in society. As part of the private sector the banks are motivated by profit and individual interests. Their investment priorities include 'speculative property ventures', and insecure fringe dealing by 'city "whizz-kids" '. Those proposing nationalisation believe that these priorities could be changed towards socially beneficial areas such as 'long-term industrial investment'. They see banks as a 'commanding height of the economy', that controls the performance of other organisations throughout society.

The banks' control of the financial sector is more powerful still. Each of the 'big four' is in a position of market dominance, although not firmly enough to prevent 'deposits being switched, for misguided reasons, to the others'. Their combined strength allows them to control the levels of their business, and of their profits, in their own interests.

Nationalisation offers one way in which to increase the social responsibility of the banks in both respects. The banks could be instructed by the government to lend in ways that would benefit society most, and to order their own affairs in the public interest.

Banking and finance

A statement by the NEC presented to the Labour Party Annual Conference, Blackpool 1976

Public ownership of the major banks and insurance companies

43. We are convinced that the public authorities in Britain must become as involved in banking and insurance as are their counterparts in France and many other leading industrial nations. A major extension of public ownership in these fields could facilitate a significant improvement in services to customers, especially to policy-holders with insurance companies, without necessitating a total monopoly approach that would serve the interests of neither customers nor staff. It would also provide the instruments the British economy needs for ensuring that the financial and industrial systems operate in harmony, jointly promoting the communal interest by ensuring that savers' funds go to support the industrial investment on which jobs and real incomes depend in the long term, instead of being siphoned off into speculative property ventures and the like. This would promote the interest of savers, depositors, borrowers, and investors alike far more than the smooth sales talk and blinkered outlook of those city 'whizz-kids' who are able, at present, so to manipulate other people's money as to make the value of the headquarters buildings of major industrial concerns appear to be worth more than the value of the concern itself as a provider of jobs and exports.

46. We propose that the big four private clearing banks be brought into public ownership, together with a merchant bank. In view of the diversity of customers' requirements, their legitimate interest in choice, and of French experience of competition amongst her three major publicly-owned commercial banks, the separate identities of Britain's biggest clearing banks should be maintained.... All our experience of managing the 'mixed economy' demonstrates that there is no substitute for public ownership when it comes to engineering a radical change in attitudes to investment priorities. If only a single clearing bank were brought into public ownership there would exist a possibility of deposits being switched, for misguided reasons, to the other clearers. This would not only render the act of nationalisation futile but increase even more the dominance of what would become the 'Big Three'. So the public stake in banking must be substantial to prove viable. Taking over the 'Big Four' is the obvious course.

51. For too long the financial system has been able to shelter behind a mystique of its own creation. That mystique has finally been punctured by the extent of the threat to confidence and to people's savings from a series of failures which now compel serious questioning of the operations of the financial system.... We must now recognise the commanding heights of the economy for what they are, and acknowledge that a major publicly-owned stake in banking and insurance is an essential condition for a viable economic strategy and for sustained recovery.

No more nationalisation

It has for long been a cherished aim of the left wing to control the banking system: then they could operate unrestrained by any financial controls, marshalling funds and printing money as they saw fit. The results could be disastrous, resulting in a yet more unsatisfactory economic situation, as funds were misallocated by bureaucratic fiat and the money supply was expanded rapidly to ease short-term difficulties, resulting in a much higher rate of inflation.

The banking sector performs many useful functions that rest upon competition between the major clearers. The function of risk management is best dealt with by competing banks, deploying the year-averaging techniques for bad debt provision. The function of attracting sufficient funds from the saving public needs competition between banks to achieve a reasonable level of interest rates and a spread of investment opportunities. The function of allocating monies to individuals and companies necessitates a competitive market place. Without competition and the need for profit there would be few constraints on lending to non-commercial projects, with consequent losses to the banking system. Conversely, with, in effect, only one national bank there would be no chance of someone unfairly refused a loan being able to borrow from another bank, as happens under the competitive system. Finally, without a private sector there would be no barrier of independent responsibility and discretion between government and the citizen. Present rules allow legitimate access to records by the Inland Revenue. However, the private banking system acts as a check on abuse of that and other government powers. With a government bank there would be little individual and corporate privacy from the other arms of the bureaucracy.

Nationalization of the banking system would add nothing to the desirable controls government and the Bank of England already exercise over the banking sector. The present network of arrangements represents the results of long evolution, a flexible system which gives the government necessary scope to influence interest rates and to control the money supply. What it would do would be to destroy the important relationship between bank manager and customer and to substitute another civil service set of procedures dominated by forms and inflexibility. The result would be misallocation between sectors and between individuals or companies within sectors. It would be exceptionally difficult for one bank operating in isolation without commercial criteria to avoid either turning down too many acceptable projects or, alternatively, incurring a much higher percentage of bad debts than is compatible with commercial success. The whole economy would suffer, whilst further incursions would be made into our liberties as citizens. Unless the national bank were given a complete monopoly, it is likely that commercial fringe banks would mushroom to meet market demands, and these would not have the experience or the resources of the clearers.

'No more nationalisation'

The proposal to nationalise the banks has not met with general support. There are powerful economic arguments to oppose it, showing how both efficiency and welfare might suffer as a result.

The banks would lose the element of competition with each other. They would no longer feel the same incentive to lend wisely to industry, to offer a good service to their customers, and attractive interest rates to the general public. Funds would no longer be used in the most profitable way, and without profitability, there might be no alternative measure of efficiency.

The free market system could continue in other financial areas. This would weaken the position of the nationalised banks. 'Commercial fringe banks' would take on the now neglected, yet still profitable areas of clearing bank business. 'Whizz-kids' would still prosper, but at the expense of the nationalised banks. In all these ways there would be 'losses to the banking system' in terms of efficient operation.

In addition there would be losses to the welfare of society. Customers would lose their choice between banks, and the protection of their privacy from the 'arms of the bureaucracy'. There would be a threat to the 'flexible system of controls' over interest rates and the money supply that has been enjoyed by the authorities in the past. In several ways, 'the whole economy would suffer'.

QUESTIONS

(i)   Suggest the economic reasons why the government should have taken into public ownership the shares of British Leyland.

(ii)   What do you think would be depositors' 'misguided reasons' for switching away from a nationalised bank?

(iii)   Suggest two other ways in which the government might increase the level of investment in manufacturing industry apart from nationalising banks.

(iv)   In what sense is insurance a 'commanding height of the economy'?

7 Public Sector Pricing

7.1 Private and social accounts

Pricing in the public sector is different from that in the private sector largely because of the social responsibilities of state enterprise. Firms in the private sector can behave in a way that maximises their profit. If they face the market as price-takers they will choose to sell at the market price the quantity that proves to be the most profitable. Those that are price-setters will decide the most profitable level of output and sell this for as much as the market is willing to pay.

Public sector firms are usually monopolies and have no direct competitors with whom to compare prices. Nor do they have a single, clear objective such as to maximise profits. Instead it falls on each state enterprise to take account of the private and social responsibilities of its position, and to set output and price accordingly.

Commercial responsibility

Firms in the private sector must break even if they are to survive in the long term. They must set price and output so that revenue at least covers costs. Nationalised industries do not meet market pressures directly, but their responsibility to their masters in the government is generally expressed in the same terms. Over a period of time they are expected to break even, setting price to cover running costs and the cost of replacement capital, and fulfilling their commercial responsibility to their 'shareholders' in government. Price is only one part of their policy in breaking even: it may also be possible to raise revenue in other ways, and to reduce costs by improved productivity. The long-term aim of breaking even is, however, one of the main considerations when setting price in the public sector.

'Rail fares up'

It is the need to cover costs with revenue that explains the rise in rail fares described here.

Rail fares up

Sir Peter Parker has one serious defect as the national figurehead of British Rail — he looks worried cheerfully. . . .

It is going to be hard for commuters worried sick by the post-Christmas bills to feel much sympathy for nice Sir Peter when he explains that British Rail really cannot avoid putting up fares on January 6.

It may even come to employing a lugubrious alter-ego for Sir Peter to bring home the realities of the railway's financial problems. And these will certainly emerge as very real indeed when the railwaymen put in their wage claims for the pay round to take effect in April.

The harsh reality is that though BR may just manage to 'beat the limits' and stay within the Government allowance for the current financial year, it will not be able to do so next year.

BR has tried to face the inevitable deficit but any action it sought to take to cut costs — or rather cut losses — is unacceptable on grounds of political pragmatism or social priorities. . . .

Something has to give. BR planned to cut 2000 miles of track, chiefly in rural areas where it was hoped buses might take over services — and perhaps the loss-making would then be shunted on to the National Bus Company.

But tourist interests have been promised that their glowing future will not be dimmed by any cuts in services at all. . . .

Which leaves the unfortunate customer as the only squeezable source of extra funds.

This is a solution much favoured by theorists and tax exiles — and the Post Office. But for BR, it is not as simple as it looks.

The increase in rail traffic over the year has been through marketing campaigns offering discounts and cheap excursion fares attracting new passengers rather than consolidating old. The new traffic has been largely during off-peak hours on otherwise under-used services — and if you try to squeeze these hard-won passengers, you lose them altogether.

This is why BR has always put more fares pressure on those unfortunates who have no alternative to using rail — and have to travel willy nilly. The commuter.

Revenue had been increased as much as possible through various 'marketing campaigns' intended to increase sales levels. Costs could be cut no further: British Rail was committed to maintaining its current level of services, could not afford the investment that would be needed to improve labour productivity in future, and could not expect to hold down railwaymen's wages.

Price was the only factor that could be adjusted, the only 'squeezable source of extra funds'.

Even then British Rail met some difficulty in raising extra revenue through fare increases. Many of their customers had a demand for rail services that was proving to be highly elastic. A rise in price would only reduce the revenue earned from this source. Fare increases needed to fall most upon those with inelastic demand for rail travel, those 'unfortunates who have no alternative' — the commuters.

Social responsibility

Nationalised industries are taken into state ownership, in part because of the social costs and benefits which characterise their line of business. British Rail, for instance, could not 'cut 2000 miles of track' because of their commitment to tourist services.

Public enterprise must make allowance for social benefits in its pricing policy. The nationalised industry involved would prefer that this responsibility should be shared by government and paid for out of general taxation. The industry could then be paid a subsidy to maintain the operation. Failing this, however, they must make what allowance they can, and acknowledge social benefits when they arise in a more generous pricing policy.

'Giveawayday'

One way in which British Rail, in common with many other nationalised industries, take on their social role is in the prices they offer to children and to old age pensioners. In part their generosity is due to commercial principles, for they attract customers and revenue which would not be forthcoming at standard price levels. But there is in addition a willingness to help groups in society to whom communication is especially important, and difficult to manage.

Sales of 'Senior Citizens' Rail Cards' bring in extra revenue that would not otherwise be earned, and 'free travel for a day' makes use of trains usually empty. In return it was 'a great day away for the old folk', and a treat that was to the benefit of society in general.

QUESTIONS

(i)   Suggest two reasons why industries that have been nationalised are in a particularly good position to make (a) a profit, (b) a loss.

(ii)   Suppose that British Rail were to increase the prices of 'Senior Citizens' Rail Cards'. Explain how this would probably affect (a) revenue, (b) costs.

(iii)   Why should the Post Office be in a more favourable position to 'squeeze the customer' than British Rail?

(iv)   Suggest two changes you might expect to see in the pricing policy of clearing banks if they were nationalised.

Giveawayday

British Rail made a remarkable discovery on Saturday. That it could profitably give away what it normally cannot sell at a loss.

Pensioners with a Senior Citizen's Rail Card were invited to travel anywhere in Britain by train free of charge.

Empty seats were filled. And British Rail sold thousands more Rail Cards — which were its profit.

Postmen who rejected a cheap Christmas mail because it might lose money — leaving the Post Office less to pay them in wage increases — should heed the lesson.

After 30 years of scaring away old customers, British Rail's policy is now trying to win new ones.

It offers so many different cheap fares that an undergraduate Senior Citizen travelling off-peak on a Thursday Awayday excursion cannot only take his bike with him free but may end up being owed money by the ticket office. Saturday's experiment had one flaw. It was such a success that many paying passengers couldn't get a seat, which wasn't fair on them.

But it was a great day away for the old folk and well worth doing again — even in the winter.

It's better that Saturday's trains should be used by the pensioners than torn apart by football hooligans.

7.2 Pricing for efficiency

'Telephone charges in the UK'

What is the price of a three-minute telephone call? The list of charges set in early 1980 is shown in Table 1, and indicates that the answer is a long and complicated one. It depends on how far, at what time of day, and by what means one wishes to phone.

How can such variety possibly be justified? And can it be efficient for a nationalised industry to set so many different prices? We will see that there are two important principles at work, both of which are applied in telephone charging. This is in common with many other nationalised industries.

Marginal cost

In the absence of other guidelines, nationalised industries must often use their own costs as a basis for pricing. Costs at each output level are brought as low as possible by combining factors in the most productive way. The firm then sets price on the basis of those cost figures. It employs resources in an efficient way while still matching revenue to costs. It meets both its commercial and social responsibilities.

But which measure of cost should it choose? The common view is that the 'true' cost of providing a good or service should pay for all factors responsible for its production. This is measured in the marginal cost of producing each individual unit. If the unit sells at a price that covers its marginal cost, it is worth producing.

The cost of a particular phone call includes the payments made to many different factors. Capital equipment is present in the form of the telephone receivers, the communicating cables and exchanges, and the generators supplying the minimal electric current required. There may even be a space satellite involved in intercontinental calls. Labour is employed to operate, service, and administer the network. Land provides the sites for telecommunication facilities, and the raw materials used to construct equipment. Enterprise is provided by the only shareholder — the state.

The individual costs of different phone calls are reflected in their prices. Calls that are dialled direct have a lower marginal cost than those which employ an operator. Long-distance calls cost more than local ones. Peak-time calls require extra investment in expensive capital equipment, while off-peak calls do not. Each of these differences explains certain of the variations in charges shown in Table 1, in line with marginal cost pricing.

The cost of a 3 minute call, from a telephone without a coin box, in the London area, effective on 7/1/1980. All charges inclusive of VAT, in pence.

| Charge Rate | | Inland | | | | | | International | | | | | |
		Local	Up to 56 km	Over 56 km	Channel Isles	Irish Republic	Charge Band:	France 1	Germany 2	Greece 3	USA 4	South Africa 5A	Australia 5B
Peak (Mon-Fri 9am-1pm)	Dialled Direct:	8	24	72	72	93							
	[By Operator (normal)]	[14]	[38]	[86]	[86]	[104]							
Standard (Mon-Fri 8am-9am 1pm-6pm)	Dialled Direct:	4	16	48	72	93	(Mon-Fri, 6am-8pm)	101	121	161	242	363	363
Cheap (all other times)	Dialled Direct:	4	4	12	32	48		77	93	121	182	242	363

Telephone Rental Charge (standard): £33 per annum.

Table 1 Telephone charges in the UK. (Charges correct at time of original publication; are subject to changed.)

Problems in pricing

Marginal cost pricing is important to the efficiency of the public sector, but difficult to apply in practice. One problem is that marginal cost is often different for each individual unit produced, which implies that a different price should be charged to each individual customer (see Diagram 1).

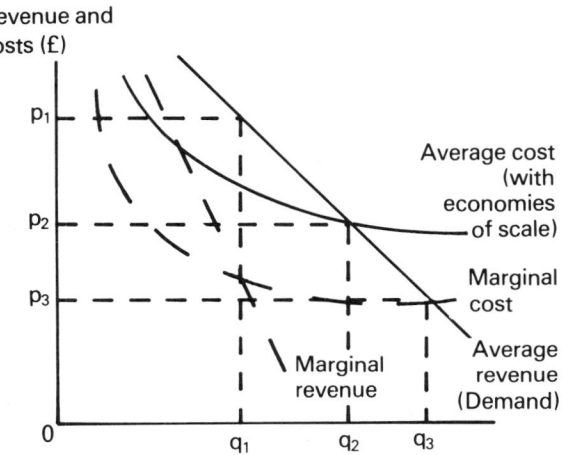

1 = if profit-maximising
2 = if breaking even
3 = if marginal-cost pricing, setting price by the last unit to be sold

Diagram 1   Marginal cost pricing

Price discrimination is not always possible, or practicable, as we shall see in the next section. Nationalised industries, however, are in a much better position than most firms in trying to apply it. Charges for phone calls can be set at different levels for different customers. There is no alternative source of supply, and little a customer can do to disguise his conditions of demand. The extent of price discrimination is limited only by its administrative costs, and by the social requirement to set fair prices.

A second difficulty arises in measuring marginal cost. It is often possible only to measure the cost of producing groups of units. Fixed costs are indivisible, and cannot be attributed to the production of any individual unit, except perhaps the very first. Is the first customer who uses a new phone link to pay for the whole capital cost of building it? Is the first household to use a shared line to pay all of the cost of installing it?

In practice, therefore, the principle is applied as and where it can be. Phone charges may differ, but to a limited extent. Distances are divided into only four groups within the UK, and six in the outside world. Time is divided into only three periods.

Even so, there are fixed costs which cannot be covered in this pattern of prices. These must be covered by fixed 'rental' charges made to those with a telephone in their home or office. In common with most nationalised industries, the phone service adopts a 'multi-part tariff'. A flat-rate charge pays for indivisible costs, and variable charges pay for marginal costs.

Spare capacity

Many of the nationalised industries are faced with a problem in matching supply to demand. Supply is dominated by the cost of heavy capital equipment which cannot be easily adjusted, and certainly not on a daily basis. Demand often fluctuates a great deal, at different times of the day. If capacity is to be sufficient at peak times it will also be under-used at off-peak times.

The nationalised industries respond to this in their pricing policy. They raise prices at peak times in order to discourage demand, and reduce the cost of investment in heavy capital equipment. They reduce prices at off-peak times in order to make full use of spare capacity.

Phone charges distinguish between three time periods. From 9.00 a.m. to 1.00 p.m. on weekdays is the time of peak demand, when most business phone calls are made. Fewer are made in the afternoons, and fewer still in the time of domestic use in the evenings and at weekends.

There are, therefore, three different rates of charges. The price of cheap-rate long-distance calls is one-sixth that of peak-rate! This protects the phone service against the need for further costly investment, and makes best use of spare capacity.

QUESTIONS

(i)   Refer to 'Giveawayday' on page 35. Why should an 'undergraduate, travelling off-peak on an Awayday excursion' be offered a very cheap fare?
(ii)   Suggest a reason why, on international phone calls, (a) there is no distinction between 'standard' and 'peak' times, and (b) only one rate to Australia.
(iii)   Comment on the way phone charges reflect the cost of using an operator.
(iv)   How should a businessman, as a rational consumer, decide whether to phone in the morning or in the afternoon?

7.3 Price discrimination

The principles of pricing in nationalised industries require them to adopt what is often a complicated pattern of charges. Different prices should be charged for different services, for different units of the same service in line with marginal cost, and to different individuals buying the same service, if their social circumstances differ. Nationalised industries can only achieve these ends if they price-discriminate, separating their customers into different groups and charging different prices to each. This is not always easy to do.

There are four main conditions that must all be met if a firm is to be able to gain from price discrimination. One is that the firm must be a price-setter in its market, with some degree of monopoly power over its customers. A firm in perfect competition cannot set price higher than market price without losing all its custom.

Second, the firm must be sure that its customers are willing and able to pay different prices for the same product. Price elasticity of demand needs to be less in some parts of the market than in others, so that a rise in price can bring the firm an increase in total revenue.

Next the firm must be able to separate its customers. Those being charged higher prices must not transfer to another part of the market where a lower price is being charged. It is this condition that prevents price discrimination from being possible in most markets in the economy.

Finally the firm must take account of the administrative costs of selling at a range of different prices. If those costs are too high they will outweigh the extra revenue which is the benefit of price discrimination for the firm.

If any one of these conditions fails to apply, then the firm cannot gain from price discrimination. Occasionally all four are achieved by monopolists in the private sector of the economy, but they are most often met in the markets served by nationalised industries. The public sector can often use the force of law to separate its market. It can rely upon the diversity of a national market, and the demand for a basic commodity, to make price discrimination pay.

The effects on the market

A private monopolist might be expected to use price discrimination to his own benefit, increasing price to as much as individual consumers can afford, and raising extra revenue at no extra cost. In this way he will be able to increase his profits to even greater levels, at the expense of the consumer.

Firms in the public sector should behave in a very different way. Their desire to discriminate in the prices they charge different customers is based on the principles of pricing that, in their turn, follow from their commercial and social responsibilities. It may well be that price discrimination, by attracting extra revenue, will allow them to set price according to the marginal cost of particular services, and according to the social benefits gained from consumption (Diagram 1).

In this sense it may be unfair to describe their

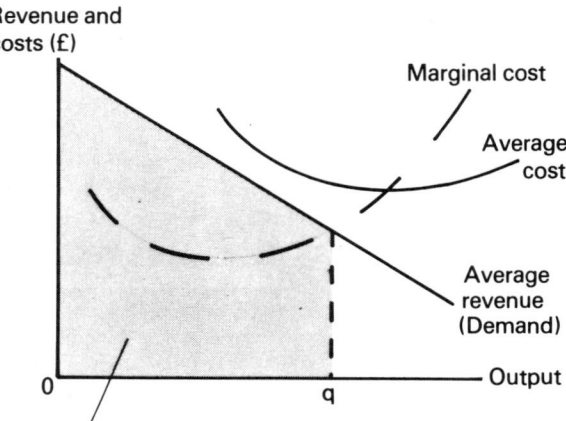

Total sales revenue if each unit is sold to a different market, at a different price.
At any single price this firm would make a loss. Perfect price discrimination allows it to maintain supply, and make a profit.

Diagram 1   Price discrimination

pricing policy as 'discrimination', since customers are being asked to pay no more than a 'fair' price. Perhaps we should describe the situation merely as one of price differences. It is unfortunate that when monopolists begin to charge different prices to different customers, whether they be in the private or public sector, they can be suspected of acting arbitrarily or for their own interests.

'Is the gas pricing system fair?'

Along with other nationalised industries, and certainly the examples of railways and telephone services covered earlier, the gas services in Britain charge different prices to different customers. The conditions necessary if price discrimination is to work are all fulfilled, since gas is supplied by a state-owned monopoly to very different classes of customers, who can be kept in distinct categories at relatively little cost.

Is the gas pricing system fair?

Sir, I read the British Gas Corporation's letter in your February 16 Business Times concerning market-related gas prices for larger users with amazement, especially the suggestion that this 'helps to ensure that our natural gas is not used wastefully'.

The facts are quite otherwise, in my opinion. The industry's own statistics give the average annual revenue for gas sold, divided into (1) Domestic, (2) Industrial and (3) Commercial and public administration. I select certain years, to save space and show the trends (in pence per therm):—

	1964-5	1968-9	1972-3	1975-6	1976-7
(1)	10.98	10.93	11.15	14.35	16.65
(2)	6.69	6.67	2.96	5.16	7.24
(3)	9.05	9.43	8.38	11.21	14.00

This shows that the industrial user gets his gas comparatively very cheaply indeed, which is no incentive to economy or conservation. The argument I have heard many times is that when natural gas first became available, the gas boards were forced into low-price contracts in order to establish a market, but that new contracts show a much tougher approach.

Perhaps this is so, but the domestic consumers have had some hefty increases too, and the ratio between the three classes does not look much different yet. It also seems that the hospitals, who presumably are in the third group, pay a much higher average price than their colleagues in private industry.

I also dislike Mr Smith's remarks about 'freely negotiated' contract renewals. If a hospital, or any other large or small user, is fully committed to equipment which uses gas, how can it be free bargaining, when the Gas Corporation says 'Here are our new terms, take them or leave them'?

It is hypocrisy to suggest that the dissatisfied consumer can switch to a different fuel, because of the capital costs involved, and one can only sympathize with the hospital authorities (and widows and every other impoverished gas user) when they read of the size of the gas industry's windfall profits.

Yours faithfully,
BRIAN SLATER,
Member, Eastern Gas
Consumers' Council.

The most important distinctions are between 'domestic, industrial, and commercial and public administration' customers, and between those in different parts of the country. Yet even within the groups of industrial and commercial customers there will be individual contracts, with individual prices negotiated for each. This is clearly price discrimination, but how is it used and to what effect?

We would expect differences in the prices for gas to be explained by differences in the marginal costs of supply and the social circumstances of consumers. Industrial customers buy gas on a large scale, so that unit costs of supply can be greatly reduced. It is 'fair', therefore, that they should pay lower prices. At the other extreme, domestic customers would probably expect to be charged most, due to the small scale, and peak-timing of their demand.

In other respects, however, there is doubt whether the gas pricing system is fully 'fair'. It does not reflect the social position of hospitals to charge them, along with other customers in public administration, at a much higher rate. It does not reflect the pricing principles for the public sector to charge more to customers simply because they can be offered terms and told to 'take them or leave them'. These complaints suggest that price discrimination is being used in an inconsistent way that may even approach the behaviour of a profit-maximising monopolist. This might offer part of the explanation for the 'gas industry's windfall profits'.

QUESTIONS

(i) Why are doctors in the private sector especially well-placed to price-discriminate?
(ii) Suggest two reasons why the gas industry should charge 'industrial' customers less than 'commercial'.
(iii) What case is there for charging established customers of the gas industry (a) more, (b) less than average?
(iv) In what sense are the gas industry's profits a 'windfall'?

8 Public Investment

8.1 Private and social returns

It is worthwhile investing in a project if it is expected that returns will exceed costs. A firm in the private sector measures returns from the sales revenue generated by output. Cost is measured in the interest paid on the original purchase, and the depreciation of capital over time.

A firm in the public sector approaches decisions on investment in broadly the same way. It must, however, take account of social values as much as private values. A project may not be profitable in commercial terms, and yet still be justifiable in the public interest, for its social benefits.

The rate of return expected from public sector projects allows them to be compared with each other, and with the costs of risk capital. Projects can be ranked to construct the public sector's demand for capital, and less will be demanded at higher interest rates in the normal way (see Diagram 1).

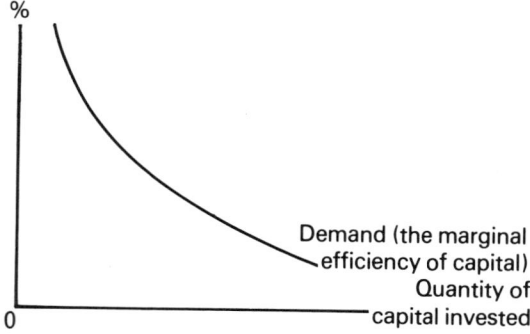

Rate of interest,
and rate of return on capital

Diagram 1   The demand for capital

It is possible to allow for social returns in all this, in two ways. One is to measure social effects, as far as possible, in terms of market prices. They can then be valued, alongside commercial issues, in a direct way.

Alternatively, it is possible to allow for them in a more general and approximate way. The target rate of return can be set at a lower level in the public than in the private sector.

'Whitby's mine of uncertainty'

This 'classic confrontation between the demands of industry and the environment' concerns an investment project which has both private and social implications. We can distinguish these most clearly if we consider the project from different points of view, the most important of which are those of 'Whitby Potash' itself, and the residents of Whitby in general.

As a commercial investment project, the development of a solution mine and refinery in the Whitby area makes sense. The costs of construction and operation would be more than covered by the returns from sales of potash over the lifetime of the mine.

Commercial prospects are helped especially by three advantages. One is the relatively low cost of labour and land in the area. Another is the scale of enterprise justified by potash deposits. The firm hopes that large-scale investment in both the mine and the refinery will reduce unit costs of production. Finally there is the possibility of 'dumping waste salt . . . at sea' for very little cost.

Social issues

The residents of Whitby see the returns from the project rather differently. In its favour there will be 'about 200 jobs' directly created in an area of high unemployment. There will also be multiplier effects on output and employment, as other residents serve, indirectly, the mine, refinery, and their newly-employed workforces.

Against this there will be major costs to be borne in the 'environmental damage' to an area of great beauty. 'The refinery would impair views', and harm the prospects of the local tourist industry. There may also be losses suffered by other firms in the area. 'In-shore fishermen' expect to catch fewer fish if waste is dumped in the sea, and other employers expect to find it more difficult to retain their best workers.

There is a clear conflict between private and public interest, between the firm wishing to mine potash and the representatives of those living in the affected area. There is one other point of view, however, in addition to these two. The national interest may also be affected by the outcome of this conflict. If the company wins its case there will be a saving to the balance of payments, and a more secure supply of potash for British industry. If the residents win their case this will protect the environment in a national park, strengthen the case of those protecting

Whitby's mine of uncertainty

National self-sufficiency in potash and 200 jobs versus environmental damage to a national park and doubts about overall local employment patterns is the main conflict being investigated at the Whitby potash enquiry, now in its second week.

The enquiry draws together many of the elements of the now classic confrontation between the demands of industry and the environment.

The immediate point of the enquiry is to decide whether Whitby Potash, a subsidiary of Consolidated Gold Fields, should establish a solution mine – that is, a mine without the conventional shafts and head-gear – on Egton Low Moor, and shift the raw material to a refinery some four miles away by underground pipeline. The refinery would be a mile away from the town centre, and next to an existing industrial estate.

Last year the National Park Committee rejected an extension of planning permission, originally granted in 1970, for the development. The grounds on which it took this step provide the text for the present enquiry.

'Damage to the character and environment of the North York Moors National Park and Whitby would far outweigh any economic or social benefits to the local community or the nation,' the committee declared.

For the nation, the inescapable fact is that, if domestic mining of potash is to take place, it will have to be in the National Park. That is where the deposits are. . . .

National demand for potash is about 800 000 tonnes a year, but last year all of this was imported, save 75 000 tonnes. Of the import total, 47 per cent came from Eastern Bloc countries. The cost to the trade balance was £30.8m. . . .

Registered unemployment in the Whitby area has consistently been running above the national average and currently stands at 661 people or 12.3 per cent of the workforce. Gold Fields is offering about 200 jobs. . . .

Whitby makes its living from three main sources. The first is tourism for which the town has natural attractions. The second is light manufacturing. An industrial estate has been established on the south side of the town which now has nine factories, the largest of which is owned by Winster Hose. It employs over 200 people to make long-length, high pressure, hydraulic hose.

The third source is fishing, an industry which is subject to some uncertainty because of the disputes within the European Community. There is also some concern among in-shore fishermen about the effects of dumping waste salt from the potash refinery at sea.

Of these three sources, the most obvious clash is between tourism and the potash development, largely because the tourist industry depends on maintaining an unspoilt environment. The opposition to Gold Fields has found its starkest expression in a poster on which the words 'Whitby by the sea' have been scored out and replaced by 'Whitby by the potash mine.'

There are two grounds for this opposition. The first is the nature of the refinery which would cover 67 acres on an 84-acre site with three buildings more than 85 feet high and a chimney 265 feet high. The second is the mine itself where there would be a network of pipes above ground and a pump house 9900 feet in area and 25 feet high.

According to the North Yorkshire County Council, 'the refinery would impair views towards and from Whitby and would be visible in whole or in part from an area of 17 700 acres, most of which is in the park.'

parks elsewhere, and bring satisfaction to present and future tourists throughout the country.

Somehow these many different issues and different points of view must be reconciled. It is the task of 'the Whitby potash enquiry' to reach a decision that will best serve the public interest.

QUESTIONS

(i) Explain how you would expect the views that 'Whitby Potash' took of their project to change, if the company were taken into public ownership.

(ii) What measures, apart from nationalisation, could the government introduce to allow the potash project to continue without social costs?

(iii) What are the costs and benefits to Whitby residents of living in a national park?

8.2 Cost-benefit analysis

'A switch from rail to road?'

How can we decide the balance of costs and benefits from a public sector investment project, and why is there so much room for disagreement about the results? The proposal to replace rail by road and bus services, over the stretch from Liverpool Street station in London to Southend, Clacton and Harwich, is a case in point. The study described here concludes that this project would result in 'an annual gain to the community of nearly £33m', but British Rail is 'unimpressed', and the Department of the Environment has 'major reservations'. To see who is right, we must ask how such a study should be constructed.

As a start there must be a clear and accurate definition of the project drawn to include all costs and benefits that will result from it. The 'rip up the tracks' study is weakened by a definition that excludes many of the problems one would expect to follow from such a project. It has included the con-

---

A switch from rail to road?

Tomorrow is the big day for Edward Smith. He believes passionately that if the whole British Rail network were converted to motorways, the country would be about £1500 million a year better off. . . . And tomorrow he publishes the detailed calculations which he hopes will convince the sceptics.

Most of all he wants to convince the Secretary for the Environment, whose department commissioned a pilot study by Mr Smith at a cost of £8938. In his report, Mr Smith urges the government to follow through with a study of the whole 11 300-mile network. Any encouraging sign will be welcomed by Mr Smith, for at present he is living on the dole in a house without a telephone.

Express buses are Mr Smith's delight, and he has suffered for them before in his 33 years. This York-shire-born graduate in civil engineering from the University of California was working as a traffic engineer for Greater London Council when he wrote a report denouncing the plan to create a new Underground service, the Fleet Line. Mr Smith left the GLC. 'They disagreed with me,' he says.

His rip-up-the-tracks study covered 160 route-miles and 65 stations between London's Liverpool Street Station and Southend, Clacton and Harwich, plus five branch lines.

He says this part of the system could be turned into dual carriageway with limited access points at a cost (spread over 25 years) of only £1 406 000 a year. He reckons it could carry up to 2400 vehicles an hour each way: all the express buses needed for the present rail passengers, plus thousands of cars and lorries.

The net result of all this, he claims, would be an annual gain to the community of nearly £33m. His main item on the credit side is more than £19m for the benefit (in time-saving, congestion-easing, and so forth) from diverting cars and lorries from existing roads. The cost of running buses would be only about £4 500 000 a year, he says, or £12m less than trains. And there are smaller credit items for sale of surplus property and for the time he claims his passengers would save. . . .

So could it work?

In the morning and evening peak hours, about 27 500 passengers hurry from or to Liverpool Street's platforms 11 to 18. Mr Smith reckons that in the evening peak hour, using 75-seaters, he could get everyone away in 382 buses, pulling out at the rate of more than six a minute. His bus terminus would consist of 30 bus-bays ranged where platforms 11 to 18 now are.

The fact that passengers would have to dodge buses leaving one bay or another every nine seconds or so struck one senior transport man as 'horrifying to imagine' and British Rail calls the terminus layout 'ludicrously inadequate.'

Mr Smith retorts that when a bus was about to go, it could turn on its headlights as a warning to passengers to halt. Alternatively, there could be a more ambitious layout with walkways down to each bay. He costs his present terminus conversion at only £50 000.

At peak hours, nine buses in 10 would travel direct to single destinations; for example, one every two minutes to Ilford, one every six minutes to Southend. Cruising at 50 miles an hour, passengers would save an average of 6.2 minutes a trip during the peak hour, and 3.7 minutes a trip in off-peak times.

Even if the buses cost as much as the trains to run, according to Mr Smith's reckoning, the conversion would bring a big gain by taking traffic off existing roads and moving it faster. On the section from London to Brentwood, for example, he estimates a gain of £13 million.

British Rail is unimpressed. It says: 'The distortion brought about by the author's gross partiality in favour of a busway solution . . . has greatly exaggerated the benefits shown.' For instance, says BR, 'No countervailing allowance is made in respect of the newly-generated traffic which will begin to use existing roads. Large time savings are claimed for the users of the busway, but no account is taken of the additional congestion costs of the extra traffic off the busway.'

And the Department of the Environment itself has 'major reservations' about Mr Smith's estimates of costs and benefits.

Things that run on tracks may still have a future.

version of stations to bus stops, and of track to dual carriageway roads, but has not made full allowance for the impact of 'newly generated traffic on existing roads'. It is expected that 2300 vehicles an hour would use the new route, but what would happen to this traffic when it reached Liverpool Street? Even the definition drawn up for conversion of railway stations to bus termini seems to be 'ludicrously inadequate'.

Commercial considerations

A large part of any cost-benefit study measures the viability of a project in purely commercial terms. In this case there are commercial costs to be paid, for the construction of the road and termini, the purchase of a bus fleet, and the operation and maintenance of all this network. There are also private returns to be gained, however, from the fares paid by bus passengers travelling on the new routes.

These payments themselves can only be estimated with great difficulty. They depend upon the pattern of demand many years into the future, and upon such unpredictable issues as the relative prices of fuel and labour. Here our study has concluded that construction costs could be assessed as 'only £1 406 000 a year'. Despite the relatively modest values involved it seems unlikely that the project could be justified on a commercial basis alone. That must wait for an assessment of social effects as well.

Social considerations

The project considered here will have effects on members of society who do not travel the new bus routes themselves. Most of these effects cannot be measured from market prices set by supply and demand. Instead they must be valued by means of techniques that are the best available. However unsatisfactory this process might appear to be, we must bear in mind that it is a question of 'that or nothing'. Either social issues are compared with private issues as fairly as possible, in the same monetary terms, or they cannot be compared at all.

As with most improvements in communications, it is hoped that this project will bring 'time savings' to society. If it is possible to predict how much time is likely to be saved by travellers, we can then put a value to that time by approximating to the price set by market forces, when labour is employed at so many pounds per hour.

The value of 'congestion-easing' cannot be estimated from the market in the same way, and here we must rely instead on the precedent set by other studies into comparable ventures.

In this case the benefits of time-saving and congestion-easing represent 'the main item on the credit side', at more than £19m. The viability of the project would, however, be changed dramatically if the estimates of British Rail proved to be the more accurate. Then there would be 'additional congestion costs from the extra traffic off the busway', to set against the possible gains.

British Rail would probably wish us to mention one other social cost which has not yet been credited in this study. The loss of rail passengers on one stretch of line is very likely to affect the level of traffic carried on the rest of the rail system. Some will decide to travel by road instead, and others might even be deterred from travelling at all, on journeys longer than from Liverpool Street to Harwich.

To Mr Smith this is a problem which he could easily disregard in his cost-benefit study. He is hoping, after all, to replace rail with road, and trains with buses, over the 'whole 11 300 mile network'.

QUESTIONS

(i) What lifespan is expected for the project to convert 'rail to road'? Why is it important to the result of the study?

(ii) Assume that the cost of running buses would be £4.5 million a year, and that 15 million passengers would be carried each year. What average fare would need to be paid to make the bus service commercially viable?

(iii) Explain how cost-benefit analysis should help the American government to choose between its plans for the control of pollution, on page 16.

Suggested answers

2.1 The economic problem
(i) Directed by individual consumers' tastes, which do not serve the collective interest. (ii) Advantage of patriotism and service, disadvantage of danger, therefore supply might be totally inelastic. (iii) If legal control ineffective, and if monopoly restricts supply through high prices, etc. (iv) Diagram 1, 1 to 2.

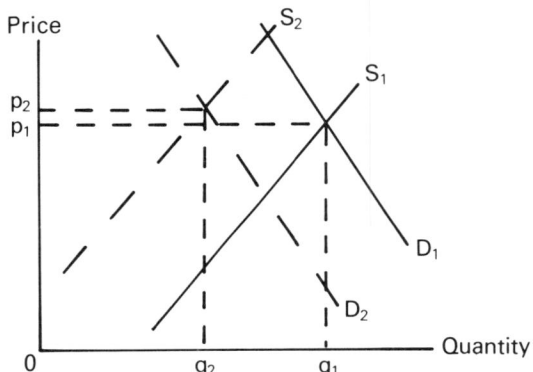

Diagram 1

2.2 Reviving industry
(i) (a) Lack of knowledge, (b) lack of knowledge about future values, lack of rationality? (ii) Lack of economies of scale, insufficient resources to re-invest, inflexible attitudes? (iii) 'Cosseting' includes subsidies to increase demand, and investment to increase supply, therefore market quantity rises, but price not greatly changed. (iv) (a) Eventually not needed; (b) continue indefinitely, perhaps even increase. (v) Groups in certain industries gain at expense of others, manufacturing industry at expense of all others.

2.3 Public goods and services
(i) Employment of others, short-term output and long-term prosperity all greater. (ii) Less risk of transmitting disease, more pleasant company, greater productivity. (iii) Public goods: benefits are shared; charity: benefits are exchanged from one person to another for free. (iv) There are social benefits, they are shared, and consumers cannot be excluded; but not all consumers are involved. (v) Because 'the ratepayer' himself benefits, from clear roads, safety and security; but also because of social responsibility.

3.1 Market imperfections
(i) Fees to clients, contributions from those in regions, general taxation; the last takes account of social value. (ii) Government-run research, subsidies to private research, tax concessions. (iii) High price attracts others in, but barriers prevent competition, therefore super-normal profit persists. (iv) Knowledge — need 'Insight' and government surveys; freedom — laws prohibit trade.

3.2 West Germany's post office
(i) Economies of large-scale production; costs are lower at each output level, so supply shifts down and to the right, and price may fall and output rise; government may favour monopoly. (ii) (a) '52% of output' allows economies of scale; (b) price-fixing, to make higher profits. (iii) As fair return for high risk, as needed for future investment, to subsidise postal services. (iv) Lack of knowledge — 'information cartel'; lack of freedom for other firms to respond due to legal monopoly.

3.3 Cleaning up America
(i) (a) Fitness, greater productivity, reduced health-care costs; (b) inconvenience to others, risk of addiction to harder drugs. (ii) Some pollution is general, and affects the whole of society, in other cases it affects only 'neighbours', etc. (iii) Demand elastic for paper and pulp, so a rise in price brings a fall in output; but inelastic for cars.

4.1 When taxes are good for your health
(i) Consumers must pay a tax to compensate others for inconvenience, unpleasantness, etc. (ii) Lower incomes spend proportionately more on cigarettes, therefore tax would be regressive and inequitable. (iii) (a) £62.50, (b) less than £62.50.

4.2 Taxation and incentives
(i) Demand highly inelastic, so high tax rates yield great revenue. (ii) Labour supply falls 0.6%, and demand falls 1.4%, therefore 0.8% unemployment. (iii) Each pound earned buys less in real terms, therefore an incentive to earn more: supply of labour rises. (iv) Rise in supply of labour, and rise in aggregate demand for products; both encourage output to rise.

4.3 Tax cuts
(i) Inelastic demand: burden falls heavily on con-

sumers. (ii) Efficient and heavy revenue raiser, falling on 'windfall' profits in short period, therefore little personal hardship or disincentive, discouraging the social cost of using this scarce resource. (iii) Tax would be regressive. (iv) If normal profits are taxed in the long term.

5.1 The problems of agriculture
(i) If price elasticity of demand greater than 1, or if government support. (ii) (a) £2.70 to £2.80; (b) 32 000; (c) 34 000. (iii) (a) A complete cycle would be longer: 10 years instead of 4; (b) farmers could anticipate fluctuations and prevent the cobweb cycle. (iv) (a) 0.71; (b) 0; (c) 0.93.

5.2 Buffer stocks
(i) 'EEC-guaranteed prices', by intervention buying to give farmers 'acceptable but low' incomes, and to add to stocks. (ii) 65 million bags X the price per bag at the level prices would rise to. (iii) Monopoly: restrict sales to raise price and make super-normal profit. (iv) Supply increased by 'record-breaking harvests', demand decreased due to changing tastes, but price maintained by EEC price system; Diagram 2.

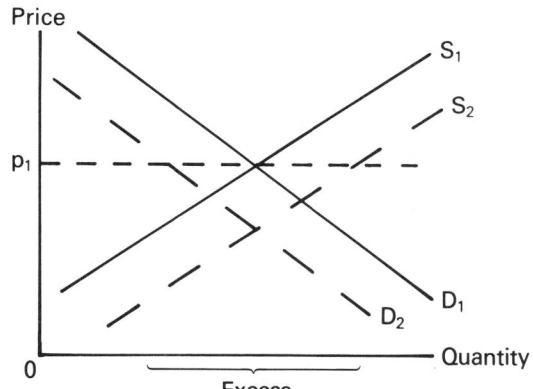

Diagram 2

6.1 The biggest boss in Britain
(i) (a) Social issues, public service, etc.; (b) profit and growth, etc. (ii) Fairey 100%, and is nationalised; Ferranti 50%, and the state has effective control of shareholders; ICL 24%, and state involvement without control. (iii) Subsidies offer less control, but more direct support.

6.2 Nationalisation
(i) Not for further economies of scale, but for the effects of a major industrial company on the rest of the economy. (ii) The fear that inefficiency in a nationalised concern would reduce their interest

rates, and non-economic issues. (iii) Direct subsidies, tax relief, financial market intervention to reduce interest rates, nationalise manufacturing industry. (iv) Probably not as a 'basic' industry, but rather as a source of funds for investment.

7.1 Railways, etc.
(i) (a) Monopoly power, and economies of scale; (b) less competitive incentive to be efficient, and subsidised social benefit. (ii) (a) Highly elastic demand, revenue would fall; (b) less traffic reduces costs, but to a slight extent because traffic was at times of spare capacity. (iii) The demand for their services is less elastic due to fewer close substitutes; and fewer social benefits. (iv) A fall in all rates charged, to cut profits; a fall in rates charged in cases of social benefit.

7.2 Telephone charges
(i) 'Undergraduate' for social, 'off-peak' to use spare capacity, 'Awayday excursion' has lower marginal cost. (ii) (a) Demand is probably more even, since calls are made to different time zones; (b) possibly the link is never used to capacity, and as in (a). (iii) There is an additional charge to meet marginal cost, but this is not the flat rate that might have been expected. (iv) Value for money, where value is measured in the satisfaction, or monetary profit to be gained from the timing of the phone call.

7.3 Gas pricing
(i) Private meeting between doctors and clients, highly inelastic and individual demands, thus all conditions met. (ii) More elastic demand, greater scale brings economies, social support for the industrial base of the economy. (iii) (a) Committed to buy gas, therefore inelastic demand; (b) marginal cost lower, because gas already connected. (iv) Natural gas was found as a by-product from oil exploration; demand has risen because of a shortage of other fuels.

8.1 Whitby Potash
(i) Take more account of social issues. (ii) Direct controls, or taxes, or subsidies, to make it worthwhile correcting proposed form of the project. (iii) Costs: crowding by tourists, higher cost of property, etc.; benefits: greater environmental protection, more prosperity from tourism, etc.

8.2 Rail to road
(i) 25 years; returns come later than costs, and continue for the life of the project. (ii) At least $(\frac{£4.5m}{15m}=)$ 30p. (iii) 'Systematic cost-benefit analysis' would assess the monetary value of returns against the costs of improvements, at a social rate of return.

Sources

2.1 *The Economic Problem in Peace and War*
Robbins, L. (Macmillan 1957) pp. 37-47

'Cannabis ban only puts up prices'
Malyon, Tim, Co-ordinator, Legalise Cannabis
Campaign, letter to *The Sunday Times* 9.7.78

2.2 'Reviving industry or £3 billion workhouse?'
Crawford, Malcolm, *The Sunday Times* 19.3.78

2.3 'Trailing to fitness'
The Sunday Times 24.9.78

'A Streetcar Named Despair'
Norman, Barry, *Guardian* 29.12.79

3.1 'Room to expand'
The Board of Trade, Central Office of Information, March 1976

'Patent law changes'
Dafter, Ray, *The Financial Times* 25.4.75

'Diazo price ring rap'
Wilkinson, Max, *The Financial Times* 3.3.77

3.2 'Is West Germany's Post Office misusing its monopoly?'
Delamaide, Darrell, *The Times* 8.2.80

3.3 'The cost of cleaning up America'
Crawford, Malcolm, *The Sunday Times* 22.10.72

4.1 'When taxes are good for your health'
Rogaly, Joe, *The Financial Times* 13.4.76

'Fair taxation'
Frederick the Great in an interview with Boden, 11.5.1772
From Zakrzewski, C. A., *Die wichtigeren Preussischen Reformen der direkten Ländlichen Steuern in Achtyhnten Jahrhundert* (Leipzig 1887) pp. 82-3
From Pollard, S. and Holmes, C. *Documents of European Economic History* Vol. 1 (Arnold 1968) pp. 143-4

4.2 'Tax cuts and tax revenue'
Gladstone, W.E. in his speech to Parliament as Chancellor of the Exchequer on the 1860 Anglo-French Commercial Treaty

'Taxation and incentives in the UK'
Beenstock, Michael, *Lloyds Bank Review* no. 134, October 1979, pp. 14, 15

4.3 'Business's turn for tax cuts'
Johnson, Christopher, *Lloyds Bank Economic Bulletin* no. 14, February 1980

5.1 'Commission members speak up for farm policy'
Jenkins, Roy, *European Community*, September 1978

'Every cloud has a silver lining'
Rose, Graham, *The Sunday Times* 17.9.78

'The pig cycle'
O'Connor, R., *Principles of Farm Business Analysis and Management* (Irish Academic Press 1973), from Fig 3.5 p. 76

5.2 'Brazilians explain why coffee will never be cheap again'
Brown, Tim, *The Sunday Times* 25.9.77

'Market set to sell off surplus wine to Russians'
Lambert, John, *The Sunday Times* 21.9.75

6.1 'The biggest boss in Britain'
Shrimsley, Anthony, *Sun* 12.6.78

6.2 'Banking and finance'
A statement by the National Executive Committee presented to the Labour Party Annual Conference, Blackpool 1976

'No more nationalisation'
Redwood, John, 'The future of the nationalised industries' *Lloyds Bank Review* no. 122, October 1976, pp. 43-4

7.1 'Rail fares up'
McLoughlin, Jane, *Guardian* 29.12.79

'Giveawayday'
Editorial, *Daily Mirror* 12.6.78

7.2 'Telephone charges in the UK'
Post Office Telecommunications January 1980

7.3 'Is the gas pricing system fair?'
Slater, Brian, letter to *The Times* 22.2.78

8.1 'Whitby's mine of uncertainty'
Cheeseright, Paul, *The Financial Times* 16.2.78

8.2 'A switch from rail to road?'
The Sunday Times 1.2.76

Index

black markets 7
buffer stocks 27

cobweb cycle 26
Common Agricultural Policy 24, 29
controlled (planned) economies 7
cost-benefit analysis 42-3
cycles in agricultural markets 25

disincentive effects of taxation 20-21

economies of scale 31
efficiency
    in economic systems 6-7
    in public sector production 31
    in tax systems 20-21
elasticity
    and tax revenue 20
    in agricultural markets 24
equity 18-19

free enterprise 6

incentives, and taxation 20-21
incidence of taxation 22
intervention buying and selling 27-9
investment in the public sector 40-43

marginal cost pricing 36-7
market imperfections and government intervention
    12-17
merit goods 10
monopoly 14
monopsony 14

nationalisation 31-3

off-peak pricing 37

patents 12-13
price discrimination 38-9
pricing in public sector 34-9
public (social) goods 10

restrictions on competition 13

self-sufficiency and agricultural policy 24
social (public) benefit and cost 16-17
state (public) enterprise 30
stocks, buffer 27
subsidies 18

taxation
    and effects on supply 20
    and government policy 18-19
    burden of 19, 22-3
    objectives of 18-21
    progressive 19
    revenue and elasticity 20, 23

welfare 7, 18, 31